Why We Drive

GOLDILOCKS EVALUATES DENSITY:

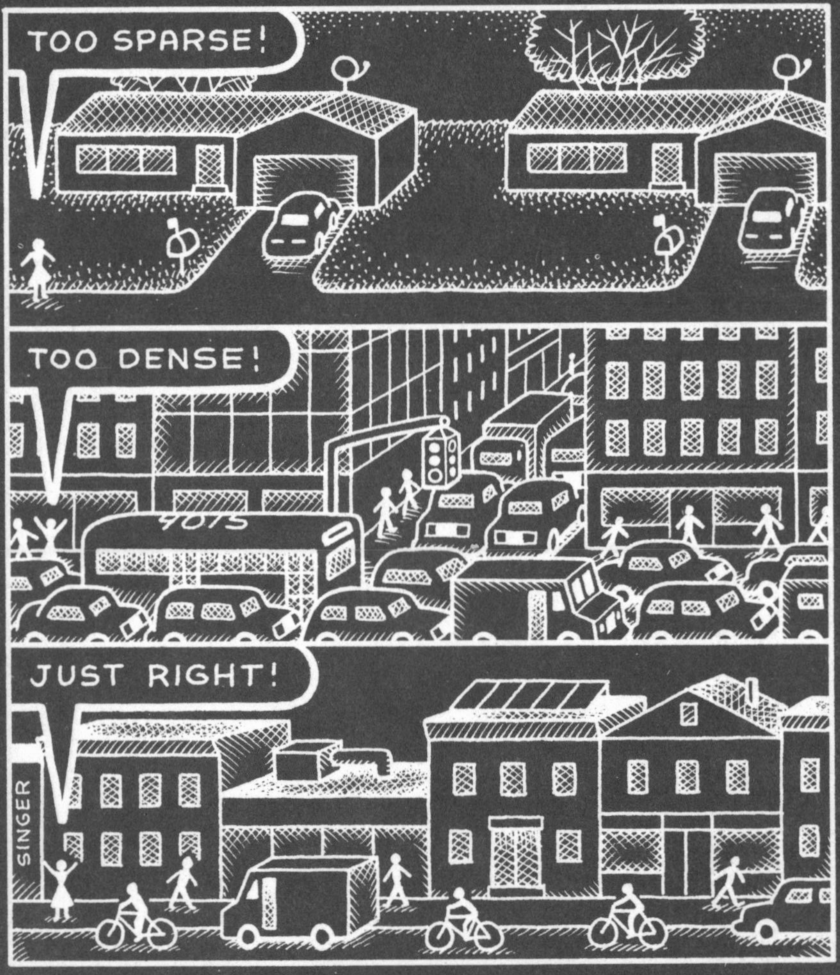
TOO SPARSE!
TOO DENSE!
JUST RIGHT!
SINGER

Why We Drive

The Past, Present, and Future of Automobiles in America

ANDY SINGER

WHY WE DRIVE
The Past, Present, and Future of Automobiles in America

Andy Singer

Released September, 2013
First printing
ISBN 978-1621064862

Designed by Joe Biel

Microcosm Publishing
636 SE 11th Ave.
Portland, OR 97214

www.microcosmpublishing.com

Distributed by IPG, Chicago and Turnaround, UK

Cover photo courtesy of Minneapolis Public Library, Minneapolis Collection

Printed on post-consumer recycled paper in the United States.

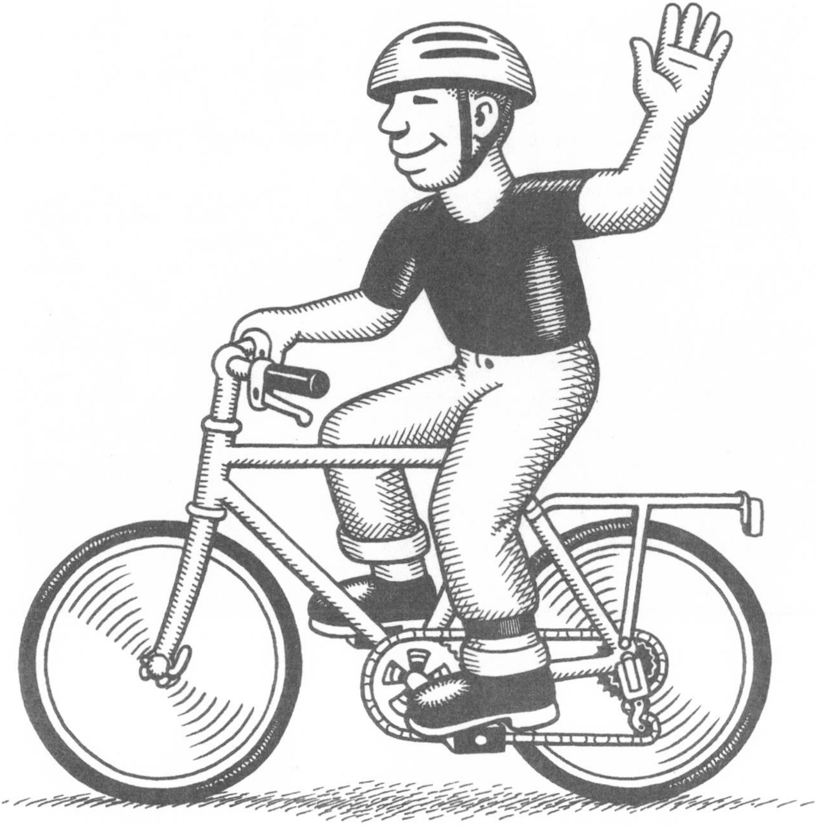

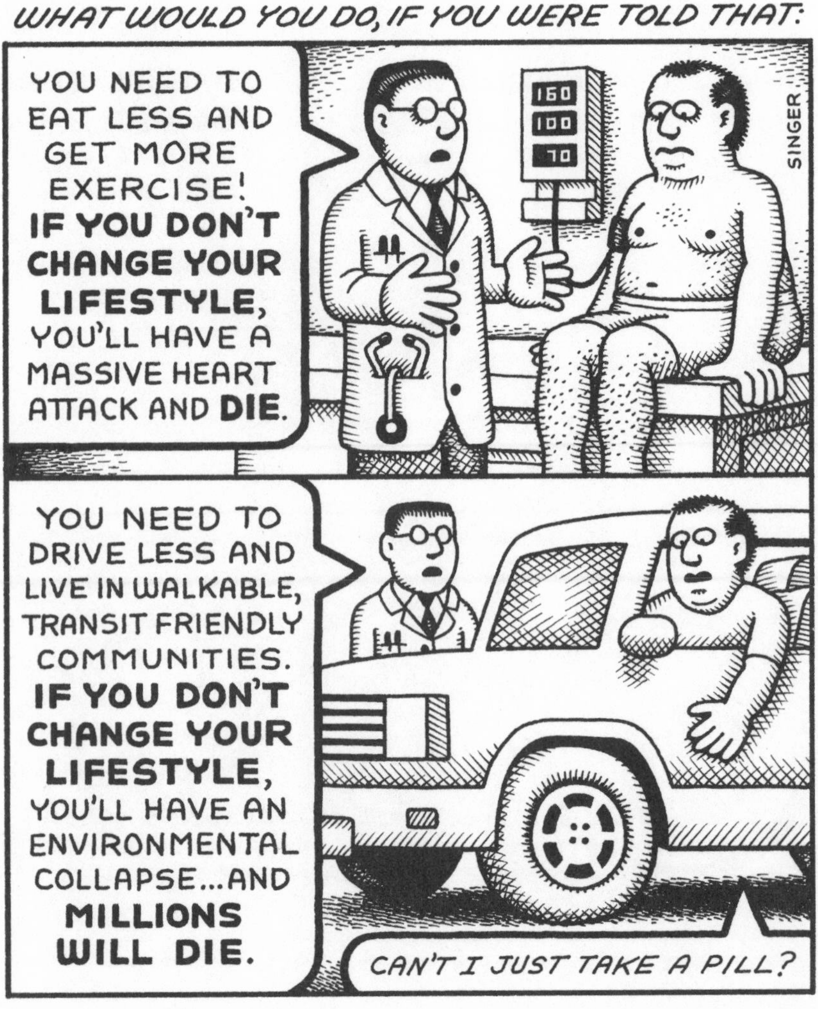
WHAT WOULD YOU DO, IF YOU WERE TOLD THAT:
YOU NEED TO EAT LESS AND GET MORE EXERCISE! IF YOU DON'T CHANGE YOUR LIFESTYLE, YOU'LL HAVE A MASSIVE HEART ATTACK AND DIE.
160
100
70
SINGER
YOU NEED TO DRIVE LESS AND LIVE IN WALKABLE, TRANSIT FRIENDLY COMMUNITIES. IF YOU DON'T CHANGE YOUR LIFESTYLE, YOU'LL HAVE AN ENVIRONMENTAL COLLAPSE...AND MILLIONS WILL DIE.
CAN'T I JUST TAKE A PILL?

Many people believe that America's addiction to automobiles is a cultural problem. The thinking is, if engineers, elected officials and the public were better educated about transportation issues, they'd shift the country away from cars and towards public transit and better land use. In reality, our country's automobile addiction has more to do with politics, government agencies, and our tax structure. For nearly two decades, polls, referendums, and increased use show overwhelming public support for better transit and automobile alternatives.[1] Yet the development of these alternatives has been slow or, in some states, non-existent. To understand why, this book first discusses the problems caused by cars. Then it examines the history and mechanics of highway politics. And finally, it suggests some ways that money can be directed away from highway building and towards non-automotive transportation.

An acronym used repeatedly throughout this book is "D.O.T." or "DOT" for short. This stands for "Department of Transportation." Almost every state has one. This is the agency that builds and maintains all your state and federal highways. If you're lucky, it also builds and maintains a few bikeways and a little public transit. In Minnesota, we have the "Minnesota Department of Transportation" or "MnDOT." Some states, like Massachusetts or Pennsylvania also have "Turnpike Authorities" in addition to DOTs. In many respects, these function much like DOTs. So, when I refer to DOTs, I'm also referring to Turnpike Authorities.

---

1   Across the U.S., from 2000-2010, of the 367 state transit ballot measures proposed to voters, 70% have been approved, double the rate of ballot measures generally. "Trends over a Decade," a 2-page press-release, Center for Transportation Excellence, http://www.cfte.org/

Leigh Ann Renzulli, "Transit Ridership Surges, Despite Fare Increases and Service Cuts," *Governing* Magazine, June 4, 2012, http://www.governing.com/blogs/fedwatch/gov-transit-ridership-surges-despite-fare-increases-and-service-cuts.html

Amtrak trains carried 31.2 million riders in fiscal 2012, the most in its history, Joan Lowy, "Amtrak's annual losses at lowest level since 1975," Associated Press (The Big Story), January 10, 2013, http://bigstory.ap.org/article/amtraks-annual-losses-lowest-level-1975

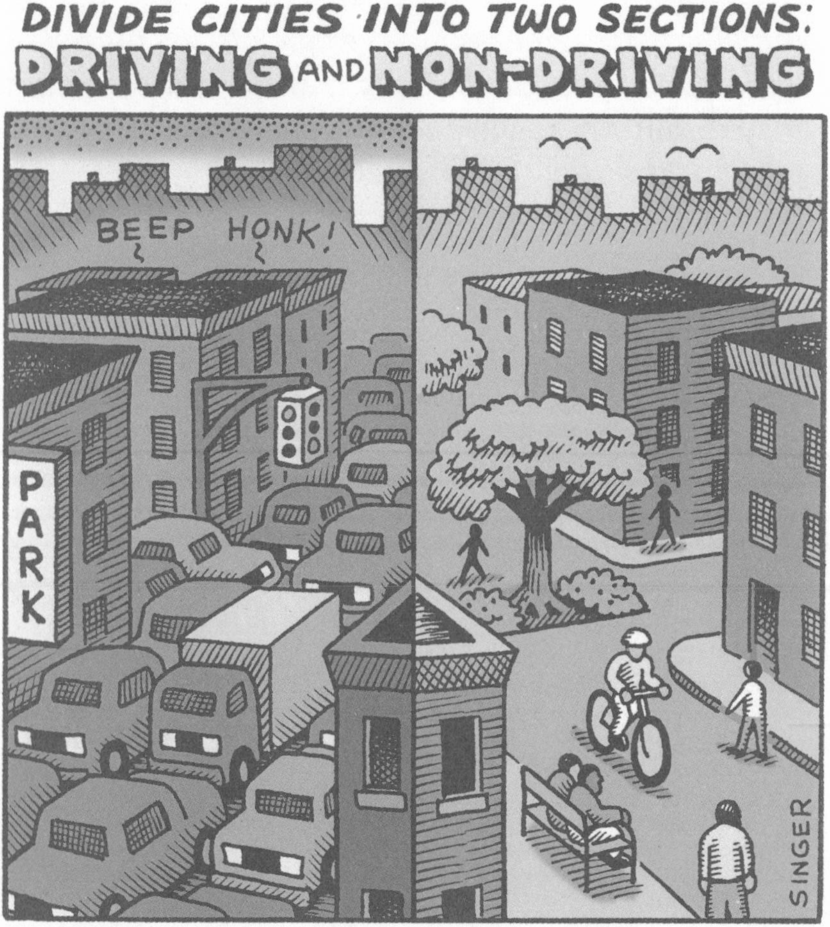
DIVIDE CITIES INTO TWO SECTIONS:
DRIVING AND NON-DRIVING
BEEP
HONK!
PARK
SINGER

I am an advocate for car-free cities, car-free city sections and car-free living. This image represents my vision of a car-free city.

You might ask: "Why would you want to give up your car?"

Giving up your car commits you to living in an urban or dense suburban area. This is because only these areas can be regularly negotiated by bicycle, walking, or public transit. Giving up your car commits you to your neighbors and commits you to collective social relationships because you are more dependent on your immediate neighborhood for employment, goods, and services. Giving up your car also commits you to behaving in a more time and energy-efficient manner, and it commits you more deeply to public transit and the environment. By giving up your car, you become a better political advocate for transit, for cities, and for your neighborhood, since you gain a more intimate knowledge of how they function.

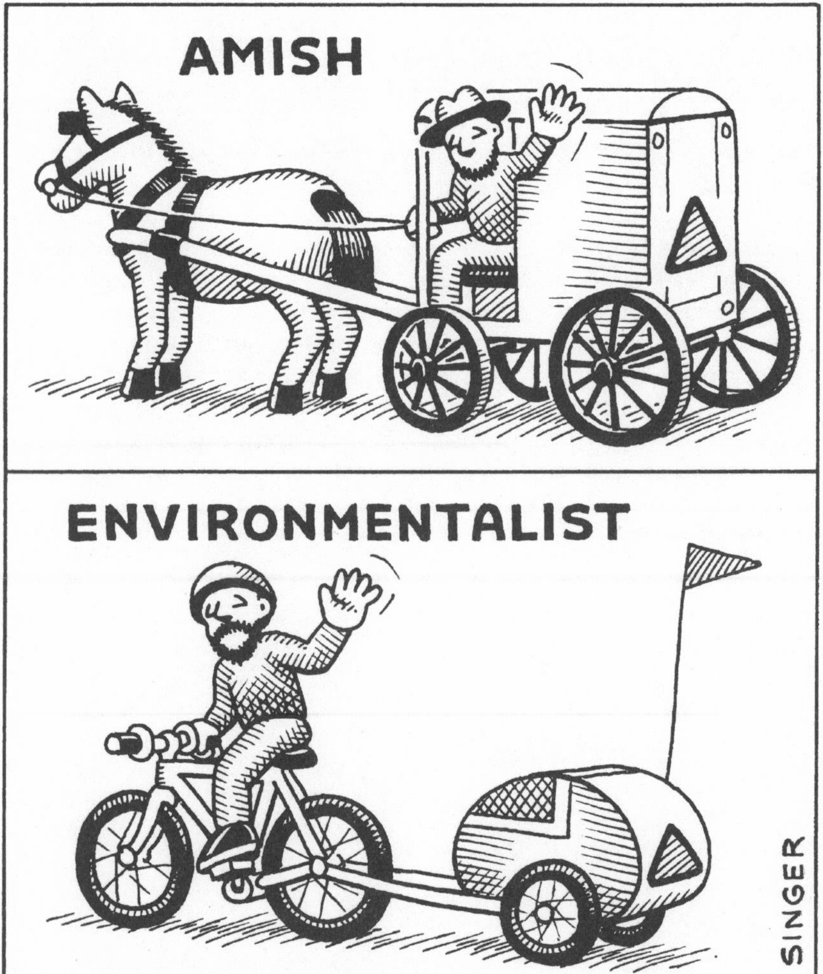
AMISH
ENVIRONMENTALIST
SINGER

Allowing your beliefs to impact your lifestyle on this level is what I would call "orthodox environmentalism." It is similar to the lifestyle chosen by the Amish. They refuse to use cars or certain technologies precisely because they feel it adversely impacts their community. Once you give up your car, you'll see more clearly how cars and hyper-mobility do, in fact, destroy community.

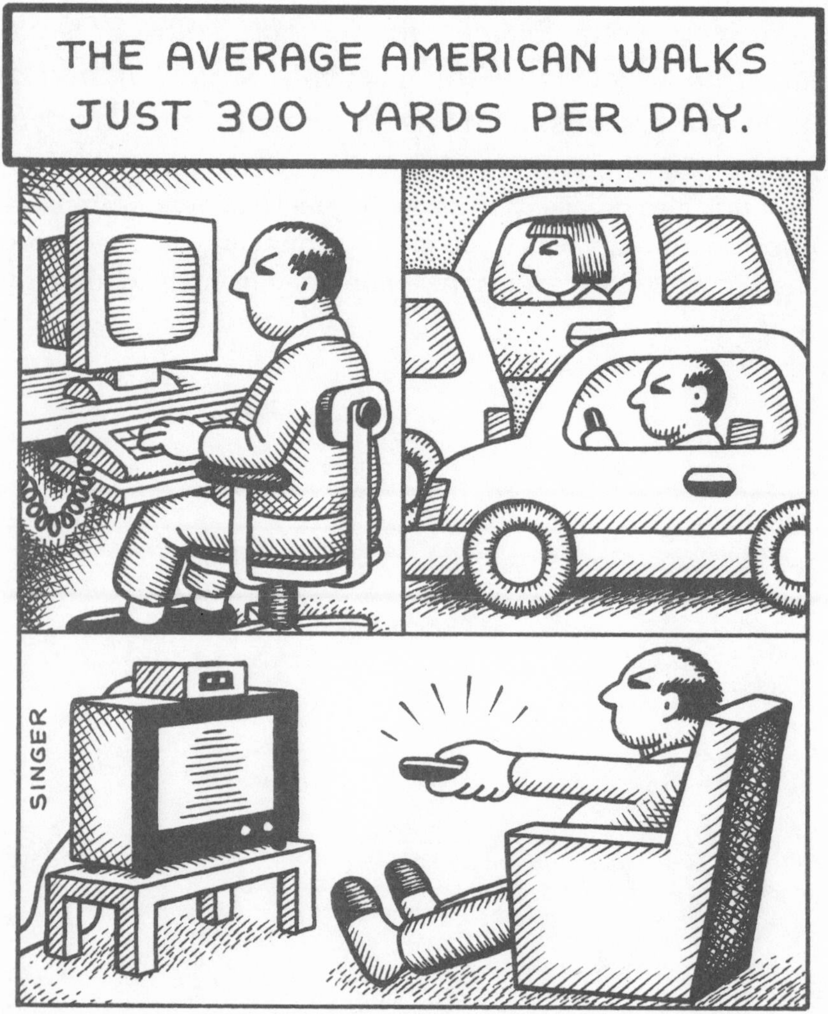
THE AVERAGE AMERICAN WALKS
JUST 300 YARDS PER DAY.
SINGER

Giving up your car has many benefits. Each year, the average American drives 13,476 miles and spends over 13 forty-hour weeks behind the wheel of a car.[2] Studies show all this driving is partly responsible for the exploding rates of obesity.[3] They point to suburbanites' increased need to drive. So, giving up your car keeps you in better physical shape and decreases the amount of time you spend moving between destinations.

2   Federal Highway Administration, Office of Highway Policy Information, 2011 data, at http://www.fhwa.dot.gov/ohim/onhoo/bar8.htm
ABC News Poll: Traffic in the United States, Analysis by Gary Langer, Feb. 13, 2005, at http://abcnews.go.com/Technology/Traffic/story?id=485098&page=1

3   Rad Sallee, " Studies suggest suburban life may make you fat," *Houston Chronicle*, April 10, 2006, http://www.chron.com/news/houston-texas/article/Studies-suggest-suburban-life-may-make-you-fat-1503194.php
Lawrence Frank, "Obesity relationships with community design, physical activity, and time spent in cars," *American Journal of Preventative Medicine*, Volume 27, Issue 2 (2004), pgs 87-96, at http://www.ajpmonline.org/article/S0749-3797(04)00087-X/abstract
Nate Berg, "Longer Commute, Bigger Waistline," *Atlantic Cities*, May 8, 2012. http://www.theatlanticcities.com/commute/2012/05/longer-commute-bigger-waistline/1952/

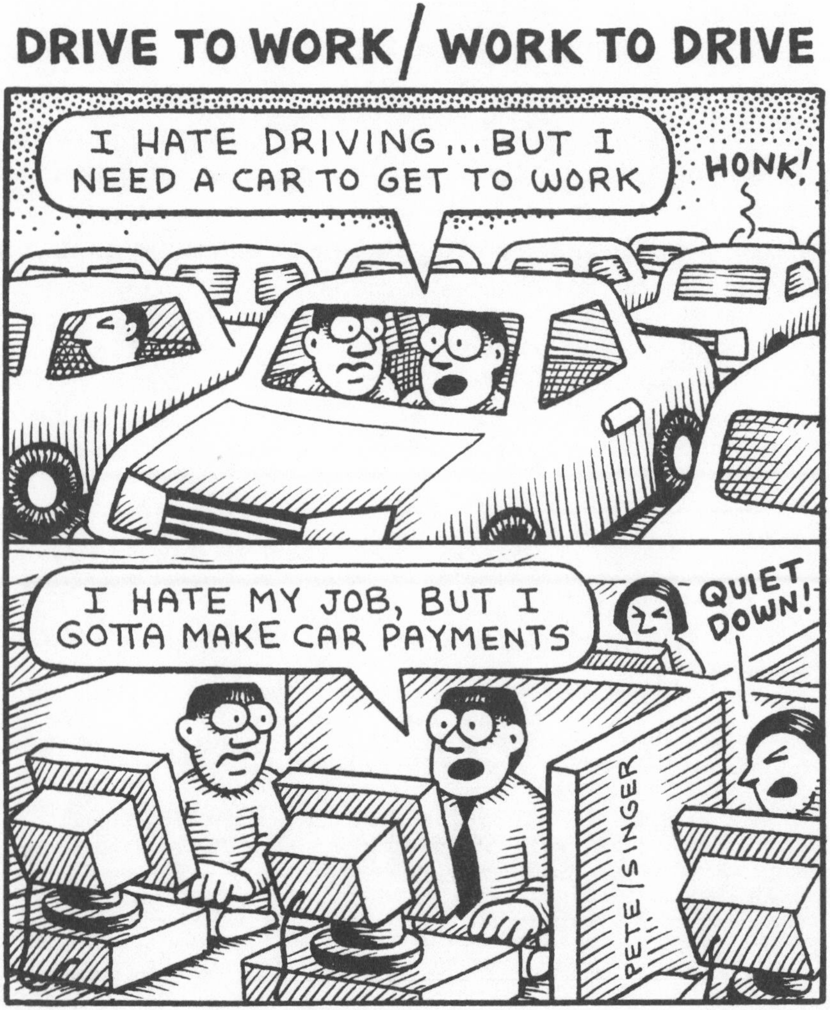
DRIVE TO WORK/WORK TO DRIVE
I HATE DRIVING... BUT I NEED A CAR TO GET TO WORK
HONK!
I HATE MY JOB, BUT I GOTTA MAKE CAR PAYMENTS
QUIET DOWN!
PETE SINGER

Because Americans spend a sixth of their income to own and operate cars, not having a car saves you money—over $7,479 per year, on average, to pay for gas, oil, maintenance, insurance, depreciation, tolls, tickets and parking.[4] As the cost of fuel rises this cost of car ownership will rise as well.

As the late Ivan Illich pointed out back in 1973:

> "The model American male devotes more than 1,600 hours a year to his car. He sits in it while it goes and while it stands idling. He parks it and searches for it. He earns the money to put down on it and to meet the monthly installments. He works to pay for gasoline, tolls, insurance, taxes, and tickets. He spends four of his sixteen waking hours on the road or gathering his resources for it. ...The model American puts in 1,600 hours to get 7,500 miles: less than five miles per hour."[5]

Today, we drive twice as many miles as we did in 1973, but the cost of car ownership and thus the number of hours we devote to our cars has also doubled. For all our money, time, and effort, we're still moving slower than a bicycle.

---

4   AAA computes yearly cost of owning a new midsized sedan at $8,780. Cost of Owning and Operating Vehicle in U.S. Increased 1.9% according to AAA's 2012 "Your Driving Costs" Study, *American Automobile Association*, http://newsroom.aaa.com/2012/04/cost-of-owning-and-operating-vehicle-in-u-s-increased-1-9-percent-according-to-aaa's-2012-'your-driving-costs'-study/

The Internal Revenue Service allows taxpayers to deduct 55.5 cents per mile for business use of a car. They claim this rate "is based on an annual study of the fixed and variable costs of operating an automobile." Multiply this by the average of 13,476 miles driven per year, and you get $7,479 as the annual cost of vehicle ownership. See—http://www.irs.gov/uac/IRS-Announces-2012-Standard-Mileage-Rates,-Most-Rates-Are-the-Same-as-in-July

5   Ivan Illich, *Energy and Equity*, Calder and Boyars Ltd. London, 1974

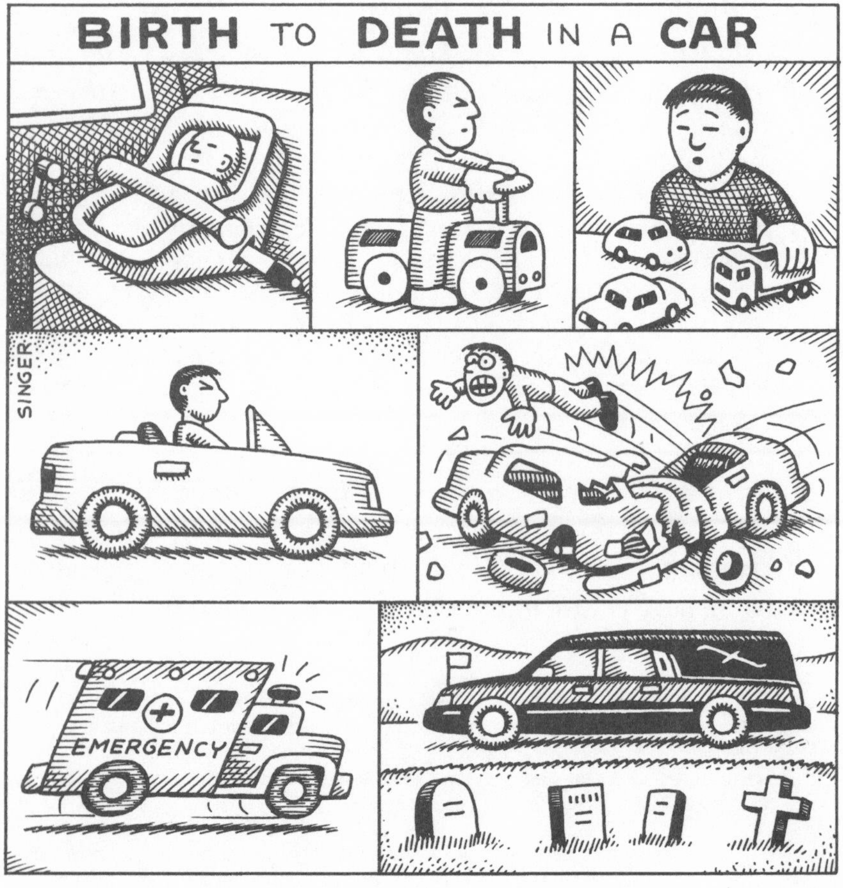
BIRTH TO DEATH IN A CAR
SINGER
EMERGENCY

Like the science fiction movie The Matrix, *giving up your car unplugs you from the Matrix of American car culture. From birth, you are unconsciously lured into the car and lured into seeing the world from the viewpoint of a car windshield.*

Fortunately for me, my father liked bicycles and trains.

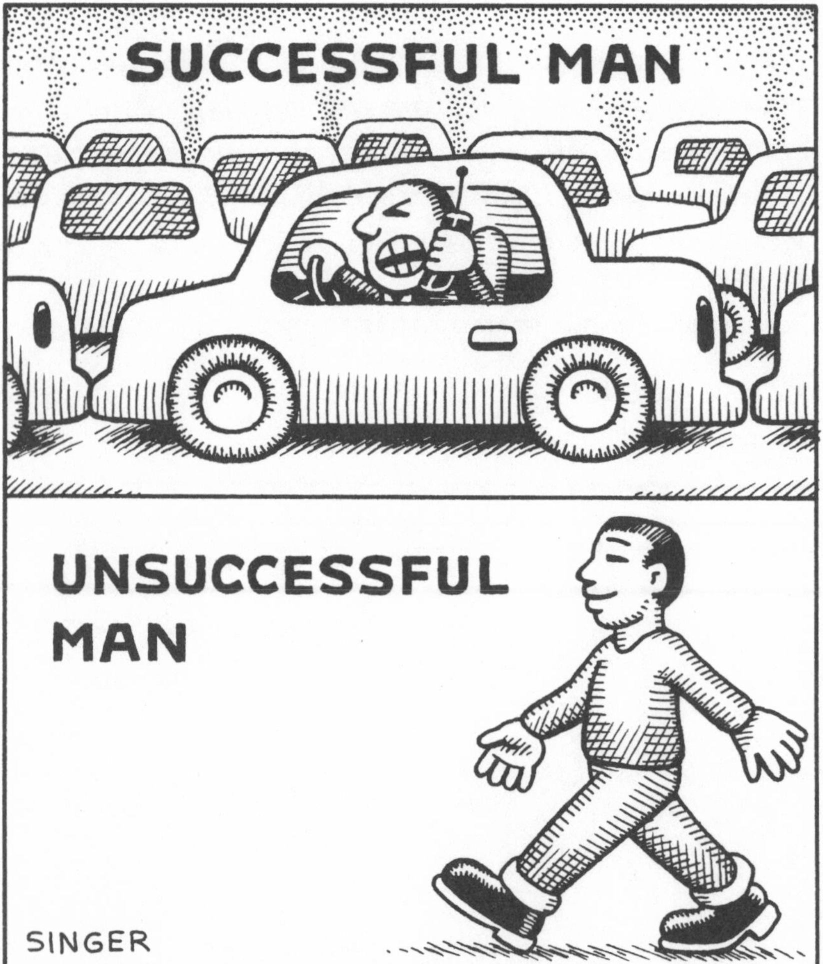
SUCCESSFUL MAN
UNSUCCESSFUL
MAN
SINGER

Cars are viewed as status symbols. If you have one (especially an expensive one), you are viewed as "Successful." If you don't have a car, you are considered "Unsuccessful."

ROMANTICIZED OBJECTS

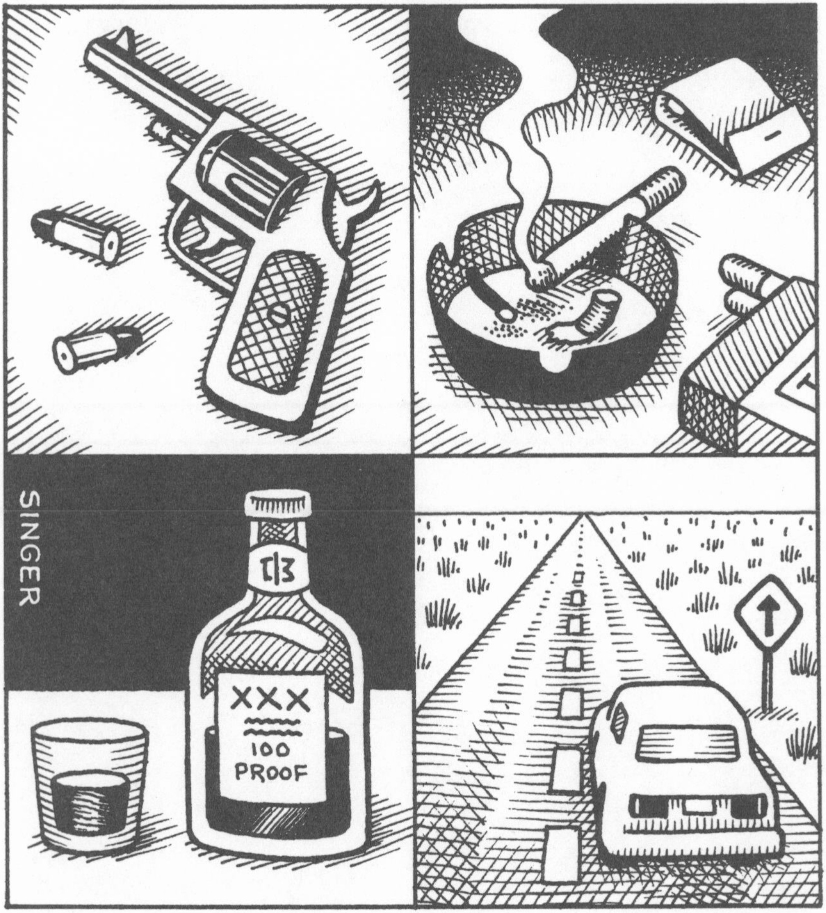
SINGER
XXX
100
PROOF

Cars are romanticized on television, in films and in popular music. There are thousands of songs, TV shows, and movies about driving, racing, road trips, and car chases. Just because something is romanticized, however, doesn't mean it's good for you. Alcohol, guns, drugs, and cigarettes are also romanticized in popular culture. But, like cars, they can be bad for your health or even deadly.

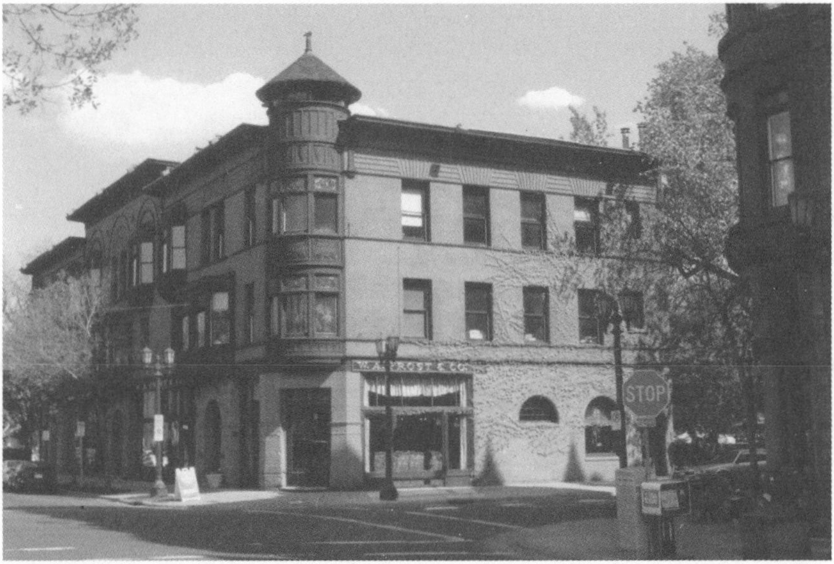
STOP

To see what cars have done to our landscape and look for alternatives, it is instructive to look at pre-automotive cities or pre-automotive city sections. These older pre-car or car-free areas are often popular places to live. The Cathedral Hill or Merriam Park neighborhoods of St. Paul, Minnesota, where I live, are good examples of this. These buildings and much of the neighborhood were built in the late 1800s and early 1900s along an electric streetcar line. By 1900, most U.S. cities had networks of street railways and cities were planned around them. Buildings were designed to be taller and closer together so that everyone in the neighborhood would be within easy walking distance of the streetcar line.

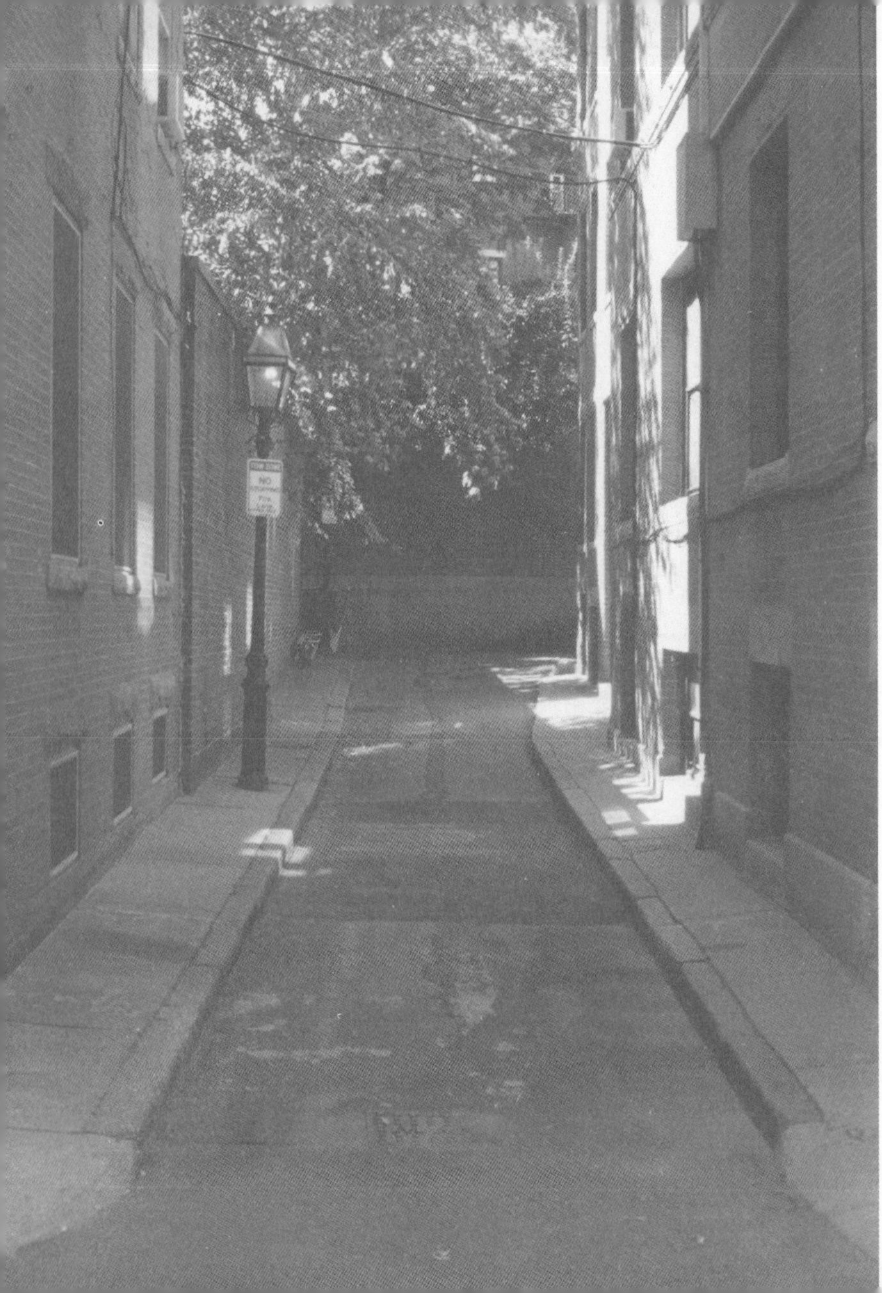
NO

Pre-automotive or car-free areas are huge tourist attractions. As my friend Ken Avidor says, even when they don't live in them, Americans love to visit places that are walkable or have great public transit. This includes places like Disney World (and other amusement parks), Venice, The Casbah, The old sections of Brussels or London, the French Quarter of New Orleans, or this spot—the North end of Boston.

Built in the seventeen and eighteen hundreds, Boston's North End features narrow streets, beautiful churches, courtyards, pocket gardens, and old graveyards...

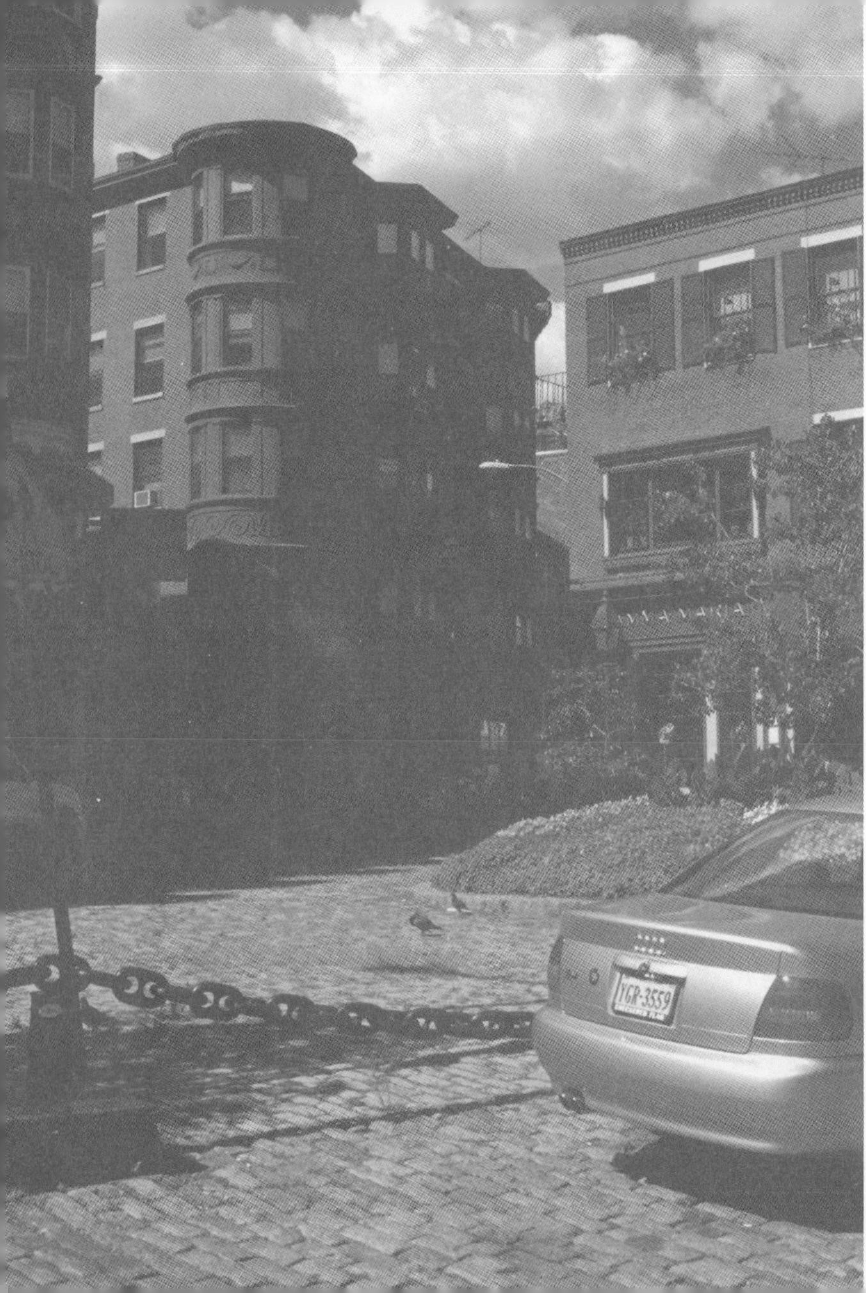

...complete with restaurants, banks, stores, and a host of services. This is where Paul Revere's house and the Freedom Trail are located. It has a few cars but no space for parking, and the streets are narrow enough that any motor vehicle traffic is reduced to a crawl.

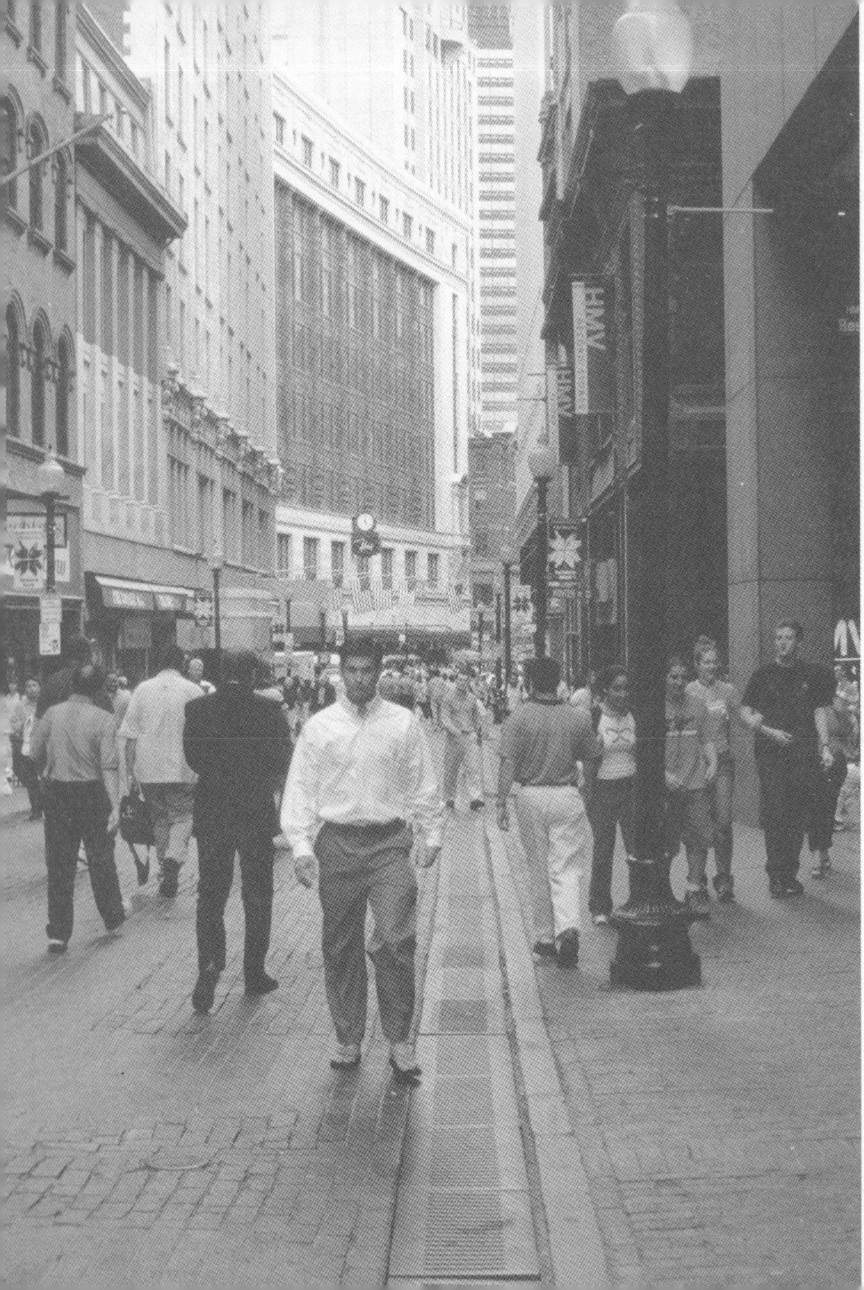
HMV

Tourists also love to see the pre-automotive, pedestrian sections of downtown Boston and the "Boston Commons." There is actually a car-free strip, 2 blocks wide and 4 blocks long, right in the heart of downtown Boston that is enormously popular and vibrant. It's called "Downtown Crossing." It's located on Washington Street between Temple and Bromfield and includes portions of both Winter and Summer Streets. Only vehicles with commercial plates are permitted in this area (for loading and unloading) and only between 6pm and 11am.

People also love the 1920s streetcar neighborhoods to the west of downtown Boston. These feature pre-automotive three and four-story walkup apartments along transit corridors, with lower density housing on the side streets. In the early days, transit, by its very nature, created dense housing, because people had to live within walking distance of the transit line. The general pattern would be a transit line on a larger street that was zoned for denser commercial or mixed use buildings, then 6-10 blocks of slightly lower density, residential housing, followed by another transit line.

You can see this transit-oriented style of housing and city planning in many of the neighborhoods of Minneapolis and St. Paul. They contain two to three story walkup apartments and old homes with big front porches. Before cars, you came and went from your house via the front door. Thus the porch was your interface with your neighbors.

The automotive suburban tract homes did away with porches. You enter these houses directly from the garage and have limited interaction with people around you. Because of the space required by cars, suburban homes take up more land and are inherently spread further apart. Thus, unlike transit, cars tend to promote low density, sprawling development and reduced human interaction.

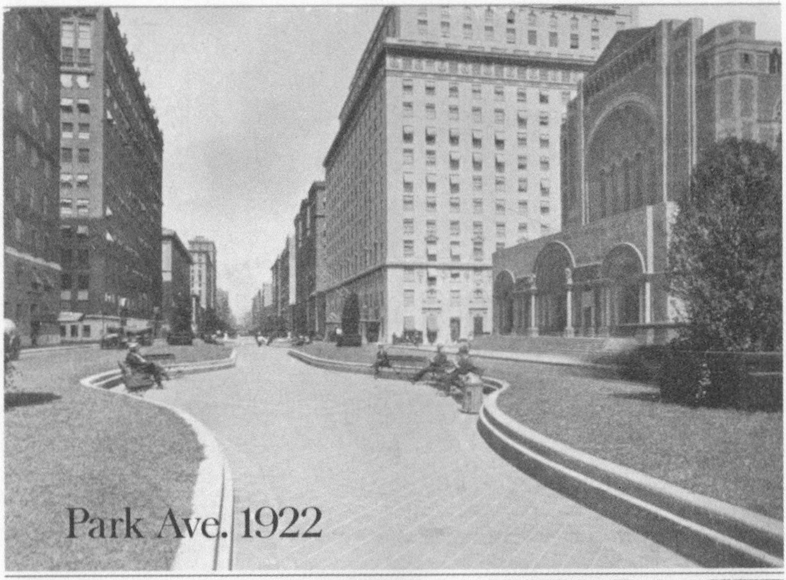
Park Ave. 1922

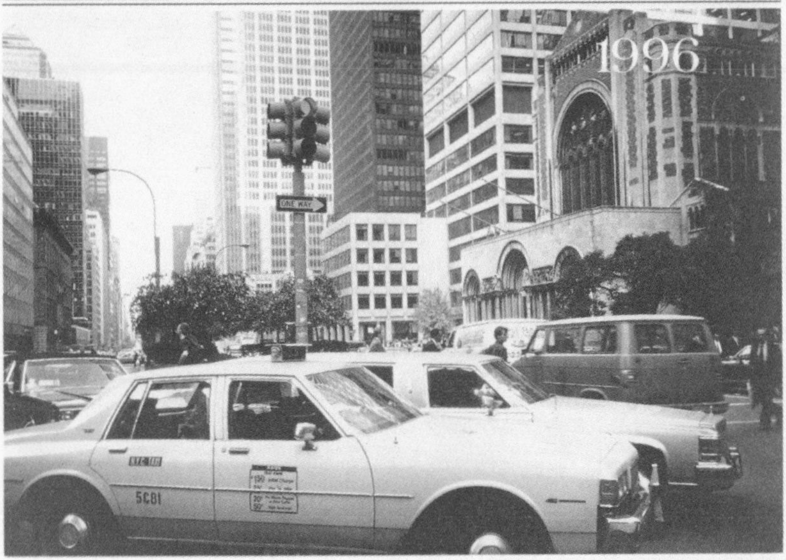
1996
ONE WAY

This postcard of New York City says it all. This is the same spot in 1922 and 1996. Space formerly devoted to human beings is now devoted to cars. Park avenue used to be a long, linear park until it was gradually destroyed to make way for more automobiles.[6]

Even in 1922, the advent of steel, electric water pumps, and electric elevators gave birth to skyscrapers and buildings that were out of scale with human beings. This made them potentially inefficient. As Ivan Illich argued that the optimal speed for human relations is the speed of a bicycle, I would argue that the optimal building size is closely-packed two to four story walkups. This is because they provide an efficient level of walkable density and yet they can be built, maintained, and lived in without the need for external energy.[7] Skyscrapers and almost any building above six stories is dependent on electric power to function. In contrast, a two to four story walkup can remain habitable even in blackouts.

---

6 Postcard image courtesy of Jeff Prant, reproduced with permission, JeffPrant.com
7 Edward T. McMahon, "Density Without High-Rises?" *citiwire.net*, May 11, 2012, at http://citiwire.net/columns/density-without-high-rises/?utm_source=newsletter&utm_medium=email&utm_campaign=dispatch

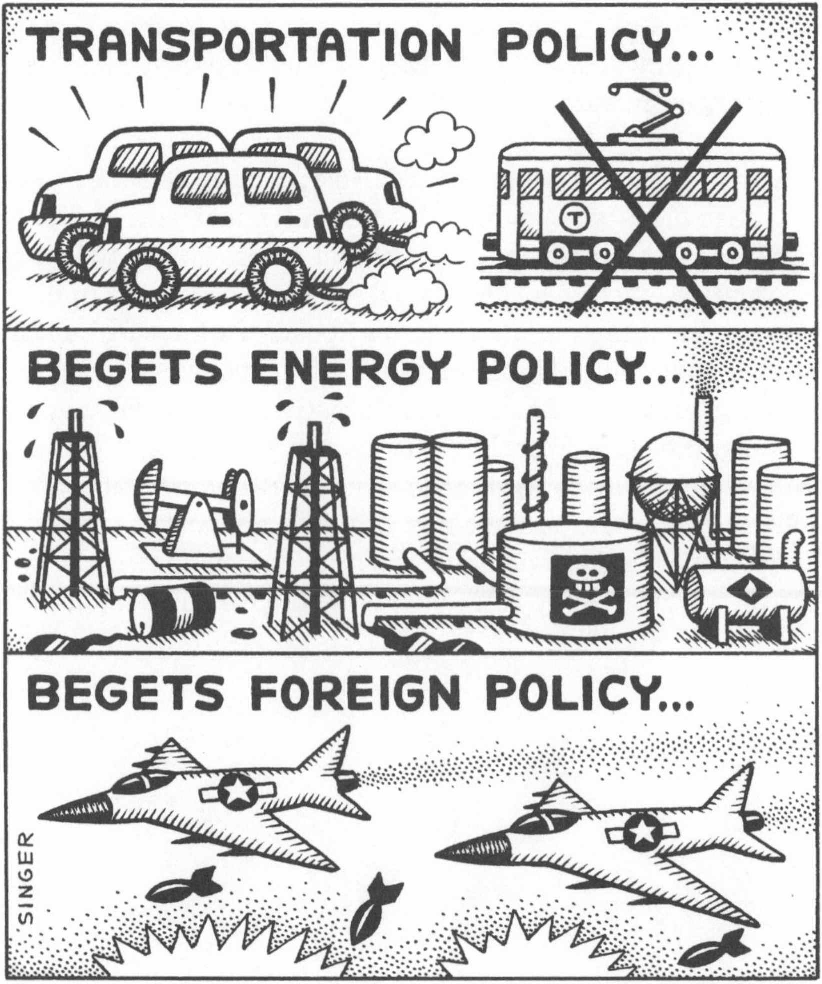
TRANSPORTATION POLICY...
BEGETS ENERGY POLICY...
BEGETS FOREIGN POLICY...
SINGER

Besides their impact on architecture and urban design, cars have other downsides. One huge downside is their wasteful use of fuel. One out of every seven barrels of oil pulled out of the ground around the world is now burned up on American highways.[8] Our need for oil is probably a major reason that the Bush administration chose to invade Iraq. Even when not at war, the U.S. spends billions of dollars maintaining a carrier battle group in the Persian Gulf to ensure that oil supply lines stay open. We've done this as far back as the early 1980s, during the Iran-Iraq war.

---

8   Albert Marrin, *Black Gold: The Story of Oil in Our Lives* (New York: Knopf, 2012), pg 124.

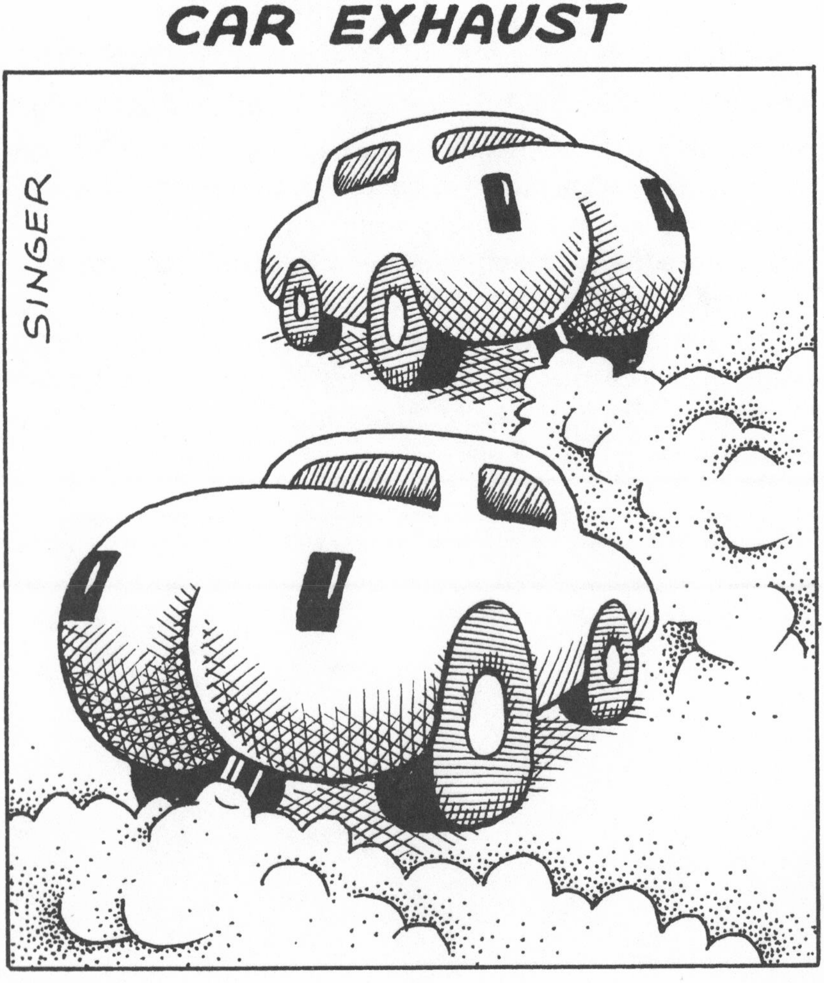
CAR EXHAUST
SINGER

Another downside of cars is air pollution. In addition to the soot that comes out of their tail pipes, cars produce "tire dust." This is a mixture of petroleum-based rubber and particles that tires and brake discs shed as they wear down. Tire dust can contain asbestos and heavy metals. If you live next to a highway or major boulevard, tire dust and soot are what blackens parked cars, windowsills, and porches. You breathe them, and new research shows that children who grow up near heavily used roads can have permanently reduced lung capacity, putting them at risk for asthma, illness, and premature death as adults.[9]

In most urban areas, motor vehicles are also overwhelmingly responsible for smog and bad air quality.

9   "State of the Air 2012," *American Lung Association*, pgs 35-36, http://www.stateoftheair.org/2012/assets/state-of-the-air2012.pdf

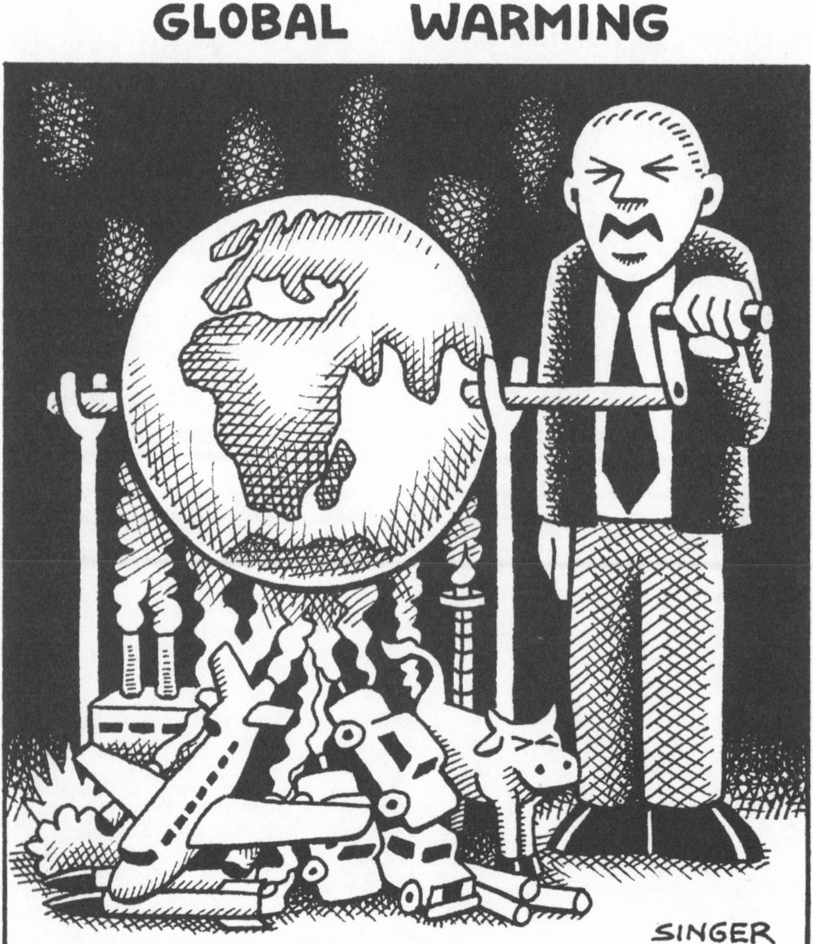
GLOBAL WARMING
SINGER

In addition to air pollution, cars pollute our water via oil runoff from streets and highways, leaking gas station tanks and tanker spills. Most importantly, vehicle carbon dioxide emissions are one of the biggest contributors to climate change and global warming.[10]

10   "National Greenhouse Gas Emissions Data 1990-2011," Environmental Protection Agency, http://www.epa.gov/climatechange/ghgemissions/usinventoryreport.html

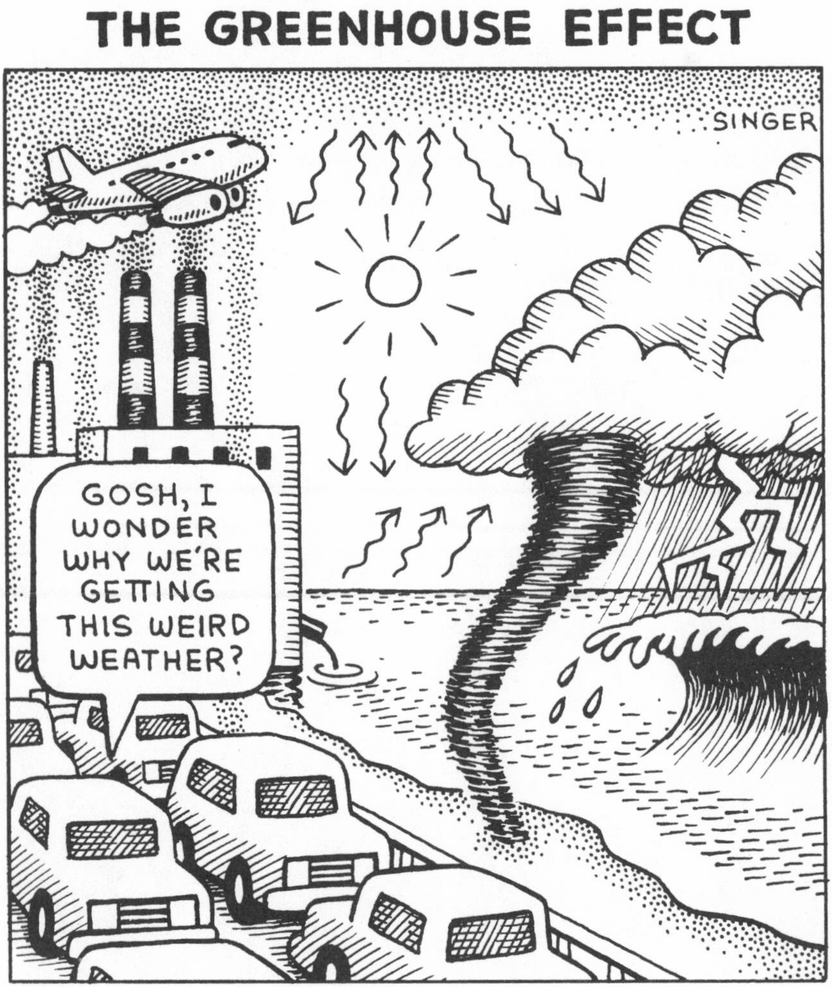
THE GREENHOUSE EFFECT
SINGER
GOSH, I WONDER WHY WE'RE GETTING THIS WEIRD WEATHER?

In addressing climate change and air pollution, the environmental movement tends to focus on increasing fuel efficiency standards and reducing vehicle emissions. Periodically, they are able to raise the "Corporate Average Fuel Economy" (CAFE) standards for new cars and trucks.

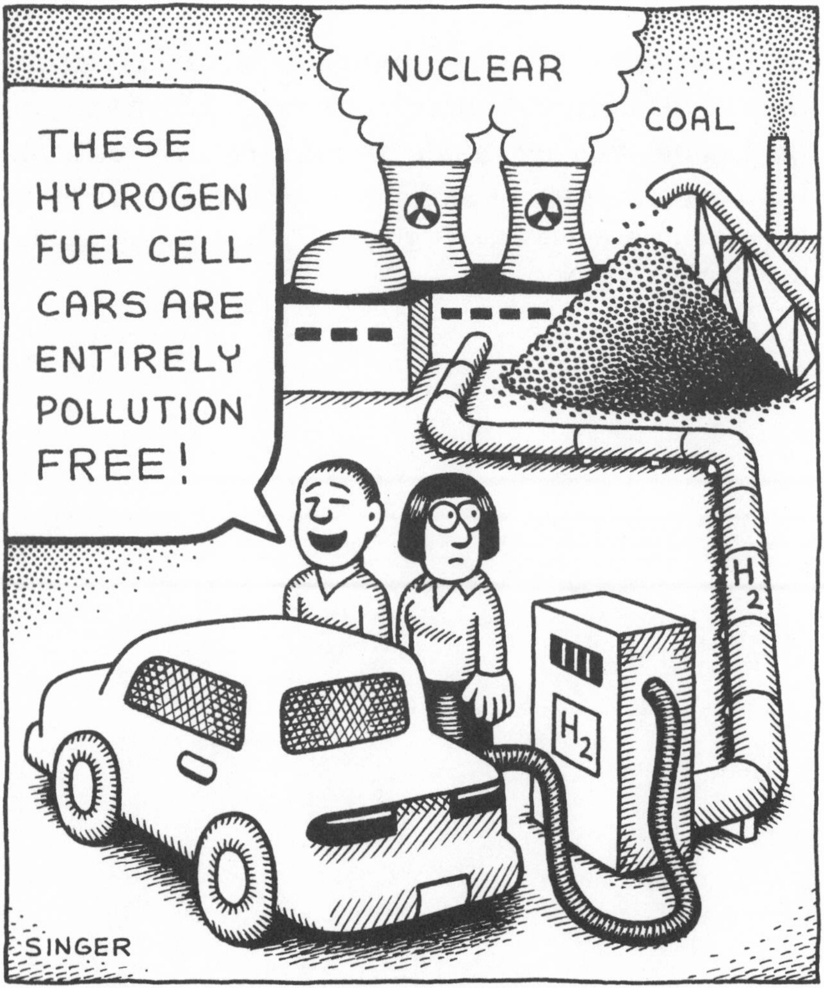
THESE HYDROGEN FUEL CELL CARS ARE ENTIRELY POLLUTION FREE!
NUCLEAR
COAL
H_2
H_2
SINGER

To raise fuel economy and lower emissions, environmentalists and auto makers tend to advocate for hybrid and alternative fuel vehicles. While hybrids are a necessary and available improvement, alternative fuels like hydrogen fuel cells are a long way off and have a host of problems.

Hydrogen is not an energy source in itself. It merely functions as a battery and offers a way of holding an electric current that is less toxic than conventional batteries, which can contain acid, lead, and other rare or toxic materials. The problem is that hydrogen is currently much less efficient than conventional batteries, meaning that significantly more energy must be put into creating the hydrogen than can be obtained from it in electric current. Also, most hydrogen is currently created using nuclear power or fossil fuels like coal, making it even less environmentally friendly.

Hydrogen fuel cells would need to be a lot more efficient and the hydrogen would have to be created from wind or solar power to have any positive impact. Such advances in hydrogen fuel cell technology are a long way off.[11]

---

11   Chuck Squatriglia, "Hydrogen Cars Won't Make a Difference for 40 Years," *Wired* Magazine, May 12, 2008, http://www.wired.com/cars/energy/news/2008/05/hydrogen?currentPage=all

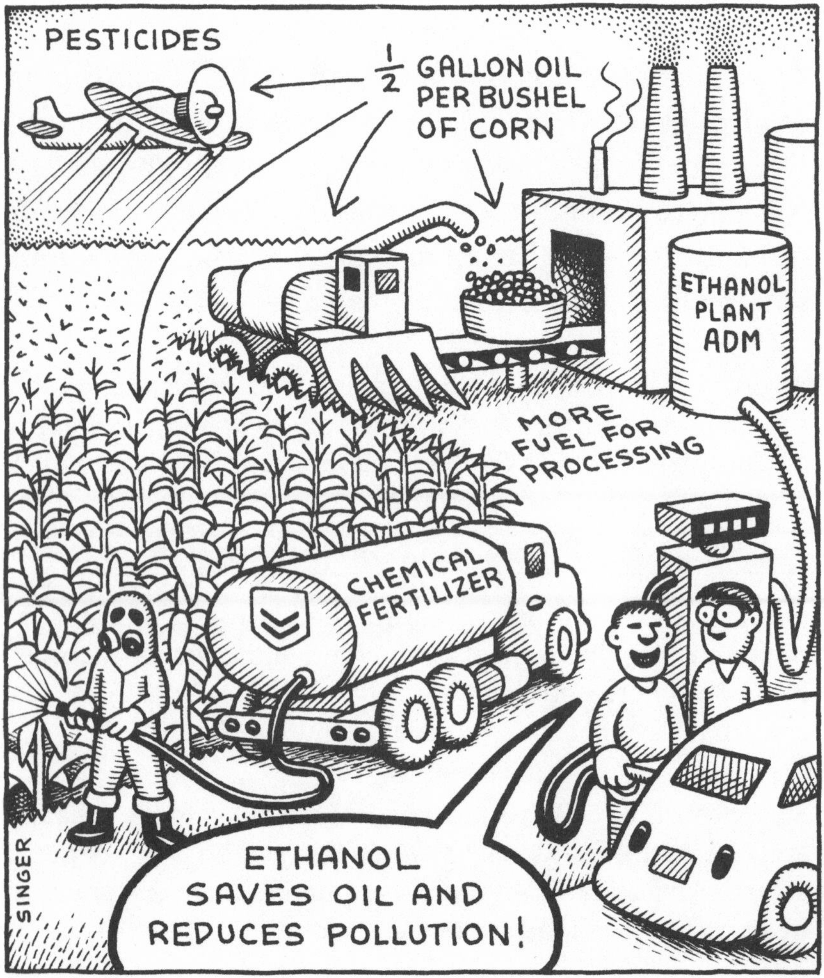
PESTICIDES
1/2 GALLON OIL PER BUSHEL OF CORN
ETHANOL PLANT ADM
MORE FUEL FOR PROCESSING
CHEMICAL FERTILIZER
ETHANOL SAVES OIL AND REDUCES POLLUTION!
SINGER

Powering cars with biofuels like ethanol has also been a focus of industry and, initially, many environmentalists. Unfortunately, studies show that ethanol can produce as much or more greenhouse gas and pollution than burning conventional fossil fuels. This is because energy, fertilizers and other inputs are required to grow and process the corn, sugar cane, or other agricultural products, and because forest land is often cleared for growing it, particularly in Latin America. Ethanol ends up being more of a subsidy to big agribusiness corporations like Archer Daniels Midland, than a viable alternative fuel. It also has the unintended effect of driving up food prices by taking land away from food production.[12]

---

12   "Associated Press, Study Says Ethanol Inefficient," CBS News, Jan 8, 2010, http://www.cbsnews.com/2100-205_162-709983.html

Robert Bryce, "The Corn Ethanol Juggernaut," Yale Environment 360, Sept 15, 2008, http://e360.yale.edu/feature/the_corn_ethanol_juggernaut/2063/

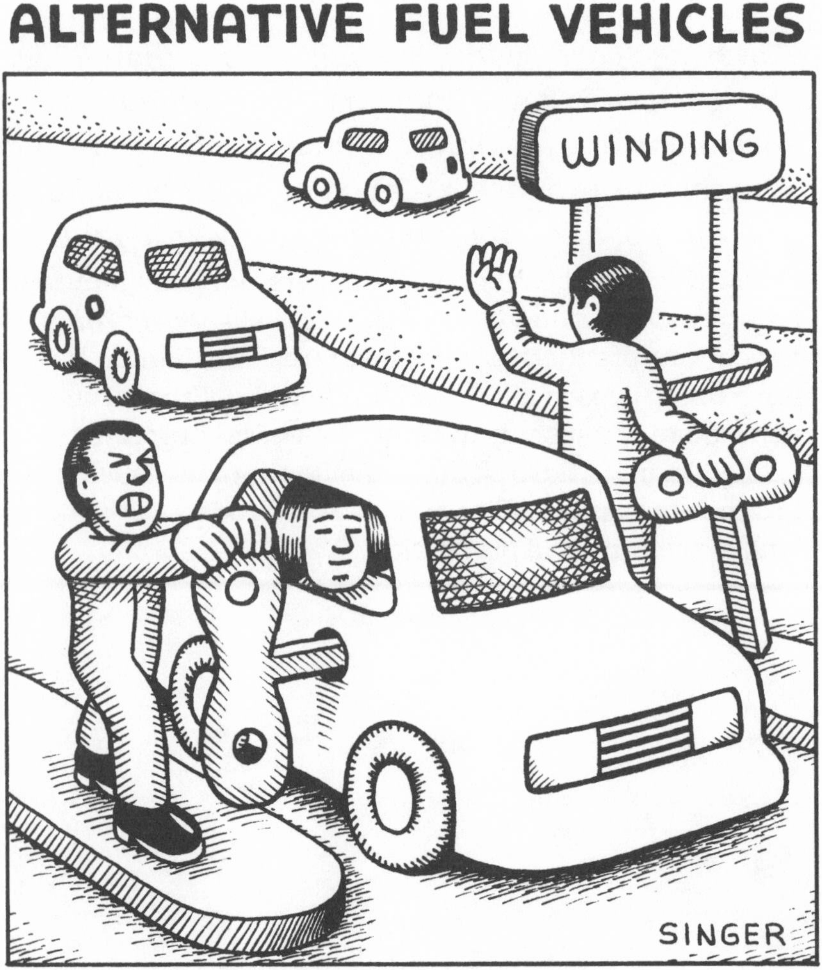
ALTERNATIVE FUEL VEHICLES
WINDING
SINGER

More importantly, hydrogen, ethanol, electricity, and other alternative fuels often ignore the fact that 25-40% of the pollution and greenhouse gas a car will emit during its lifetime doesn't come out of its tailpipe. Instead, it comes from the car's manufacture and disposal. The iron, nickle, aluminum, and other metals in a car's frame and engine require huge amounts of energy to mine and forge. The plastics in its body, interior, and tires all use petroleum. While newer electric and hybrid vehicles might have lower tailpipe emissions, their batteries and components are made from more energy intensive materials. This increases their CO_2 and pollution emissions during manufacturing, recycling, and disposal.[13]

The cement and asphalt in highways also need huge amounts of energy and fossil fuels to grind, heat, transport, and spread. Cement production alone is responsible for 5% of the world's CO_2 emissions.[14] It's the same thing with the steel in bridges, overpasses, and other highway components. If you include the energy and CO_2 emissions from road building and maintenance, more than half of motor vehicle pollution and greenhouse gas is an inherent part of building, maintaining, and disposing of vehicles and roads. Alternative fuels won't change that, even if they manage to reduce or eliminate tail pipe emissions.

13   Jane Patterson, Marcus Alexander, Adam Gurr, "Preparing for a Life Cycle CO_2 Measure," Ricardo (for the Low Carbon Vehicle Partnership), August 25, 2011, available at: http://www.lowcvp.org.uk/resources-library/reports-and-studies.asp?pg=%203

Gregory Launay, "Life-Cycle Assessment in the automotive industry," Aug. 25, 2012, http://www.gnesg.com/index.php?option=com_content&view=article&id=88:life-cycle-assesment-in-the-automotive-industry&catid=27:les-chiffres-de-lautomobile&Itemid=53

14   David Adam, "The unheralded polluter: cement industry comes clean on its impact," The Guardian, October 11, 2007, http://www.guardian.co.uk/environment/2007/oct/12/climatechange

More than emissions and fuel use, however, the biggest problem posed by cars is that they waste so much physical space. The average car uses 90 square feet of space in one's home, 90 square feet of space at various destinations, 180 square feet of road surface at each location for maneuvering and 60 square feet of space to be sold, repaired, and maintained. Thus, 30 to 50% of urban American land is paved over to accommodate cars. In Los Angeles, 60% of the city is paved. In Houston Texas, the amount of asphalt is 30 car spaces per resident.[15] The automobile's need for space literally destroys urban areas!

This 2004 photograph of downtown Minneapolis, Minnesota illustrates this. The need for car parking and driving has virtually eliminated the downtown itself and it has helped create "Urban Dead Zones," where no one lives. They only house office space, sports facilities, and acres upon acres of parking. This is typical of most American downtowns.

---

15   Jean Robert, *Le Temps Qu'on Nous Vole* (Paris: Seuil 1980)
Jane Holtz Kay, *Asphalt Nation* (Berkeley: University of California Press, 1997), pg 63-64

This is a photograph I took of downtown St. Paul, Minnesota on a Sunday afternoon. Not a soul is using this vast space—not even many cars.

You can't see this from the photo, but to either side of me are surface parking lots. So, surrounding a downtown urban intersection, you have three surface and one elevated parking lot. If this space was instead used for housing, then people wouldn't have to commute to downtown. They could live right in it!

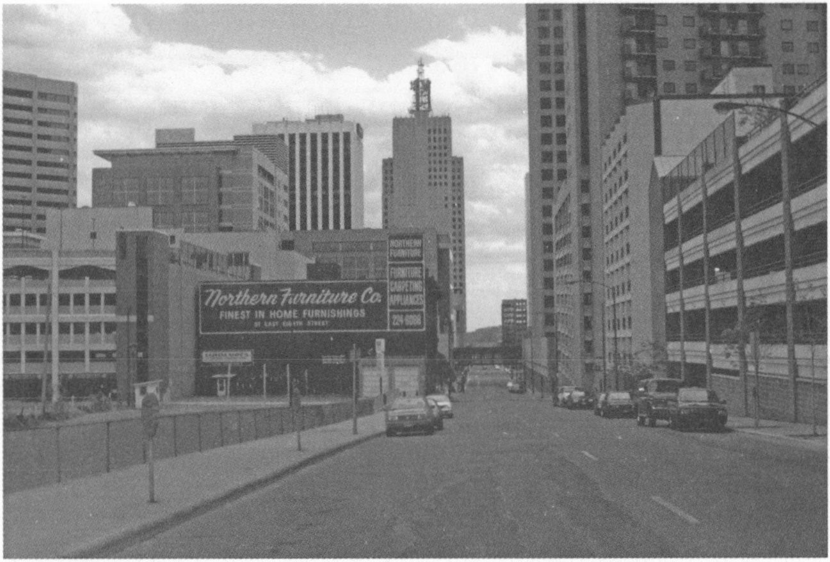
Northern Furniture Co.
FINEST IN HOME FURNISHINGS

This is another photograph of downtown Saint Paul taken on the same Sunday afternoon. Few businesses are open and almost no cultural activities are taking place.

Once again notice the surface and multi-story parking lots on land that could be used for housing, office space, or retail stores.

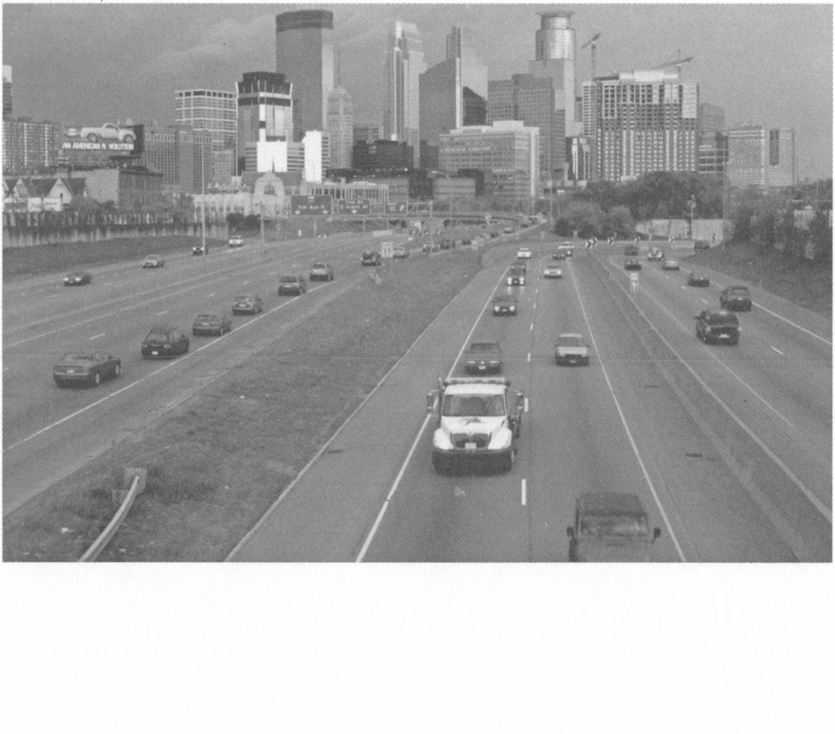

Highways, streets, and parking lots destroy a city's property tax base by eliminating taxable property— property that pays for schools, public safety, libraries, and health services. Whenever I look at a highway or parking lot, I consider what formerly existed on the land it now occupies and what could exist.

This is a photograph of Interstate 35W approaching downtown Minneapolis. Large townhomes and apartment buildings formerly occupied the land underneath this freeway. They represented millions of dollars in annual property tax revenue.

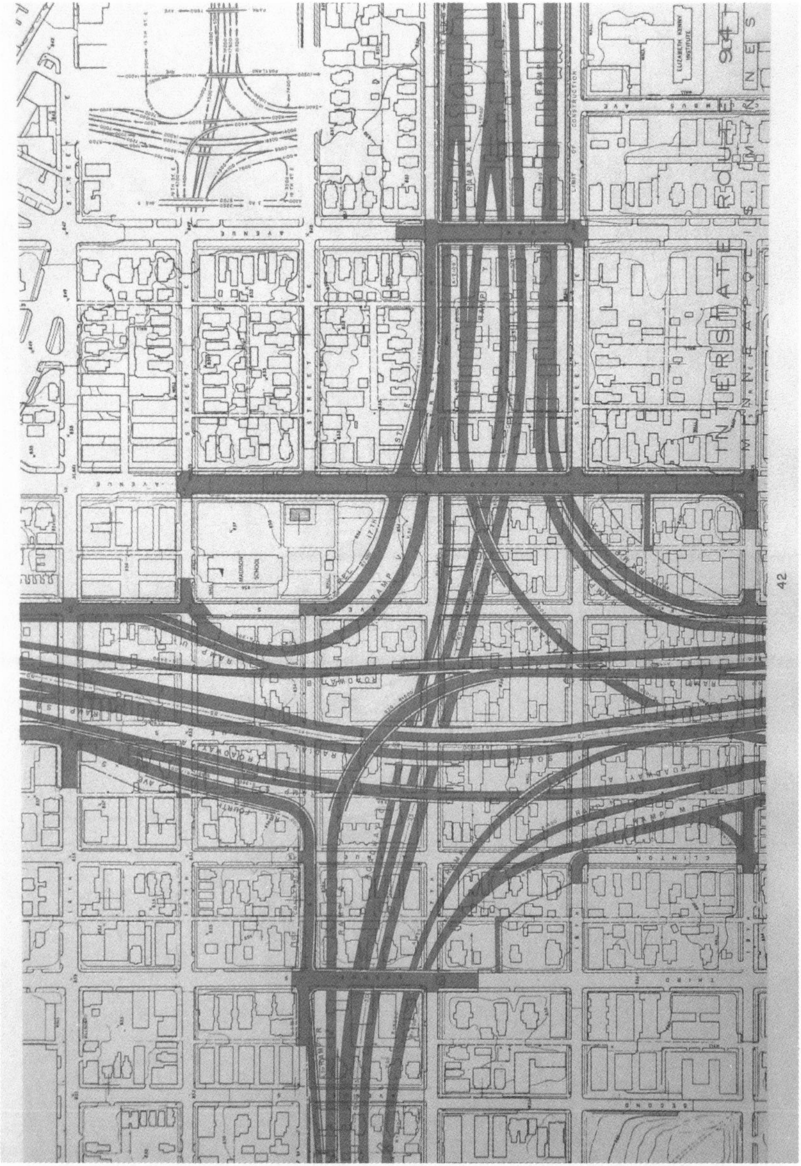

INTERSTATE ROUTE 94
MINNEAPOLIS
42

To illustrate this loss of property tax revenue and space more graphically, here is a map, prepared by the Minnesota Department of Transportation in 1953. It shows just one section of the then "proposed" Interstate 35 that MnDOT ripped through the heart of downtown Minneapolis. You can see each property that had to be destroyed for this interchange—over one hundred and fifty properties, just for this one section.

Very conservatively, let's assume an average property tax of $3,500 per building, per year. Multiply that by the hundred and fifty properties destroyed on this section of highway and the loss of property tax for this section is more than $525,000 per year!

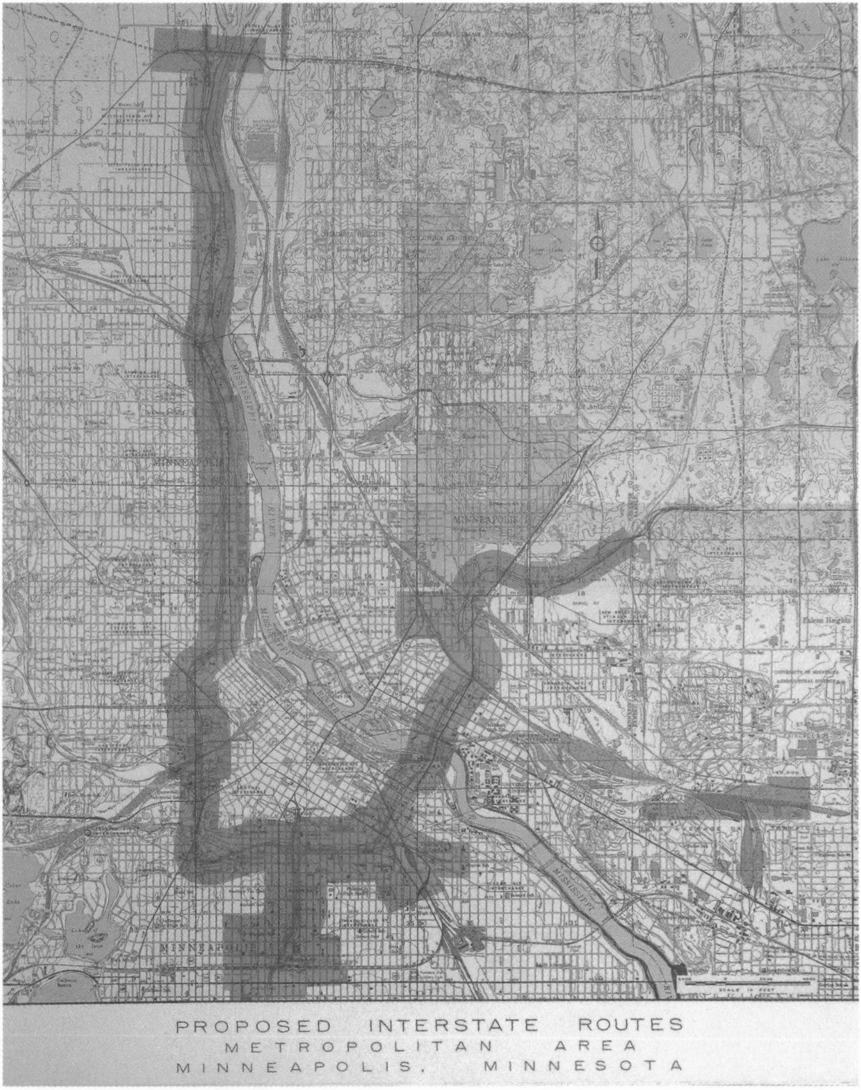
MISSISSIPPI
RIVER
MINNEAPOLIS
Falcon Heights
Lauderdale

PROPOSED INTERSTATE ROUTES
METROPOLITAN AREA
MINNEAPOLIS, MINNESOTA

Now multiply that section by at least a hundred, for Interstates 35, 94, 610, State Highway 55 and all the other highways in Minneapolis, and you'll see that, conservatively, the city loses at least $52,500,000 in property tax revenue each year!

The aforementioned freeways were but a few of the major highways that DOTs ripped through American cities after World War II. They physically and financially gutted the cities and fueled an explosion of driving, suburban sprawl, and U.S. oil consumption.

Taxpayers had to pay hundreds of billions (in today's dollars) to compensate the families and businesses who lost their property and they paid billions more in lost property tax revenues in the decades since these freeways were built.

In the last 20 years, Portland (Oregon), Milwaukee, San Francisco and other cities have been able to make money by tearing down old freeways and not replacing them. They're able to put real estate on some or all of the property the freeways formerly occupied and thus recover some of their property tax base.

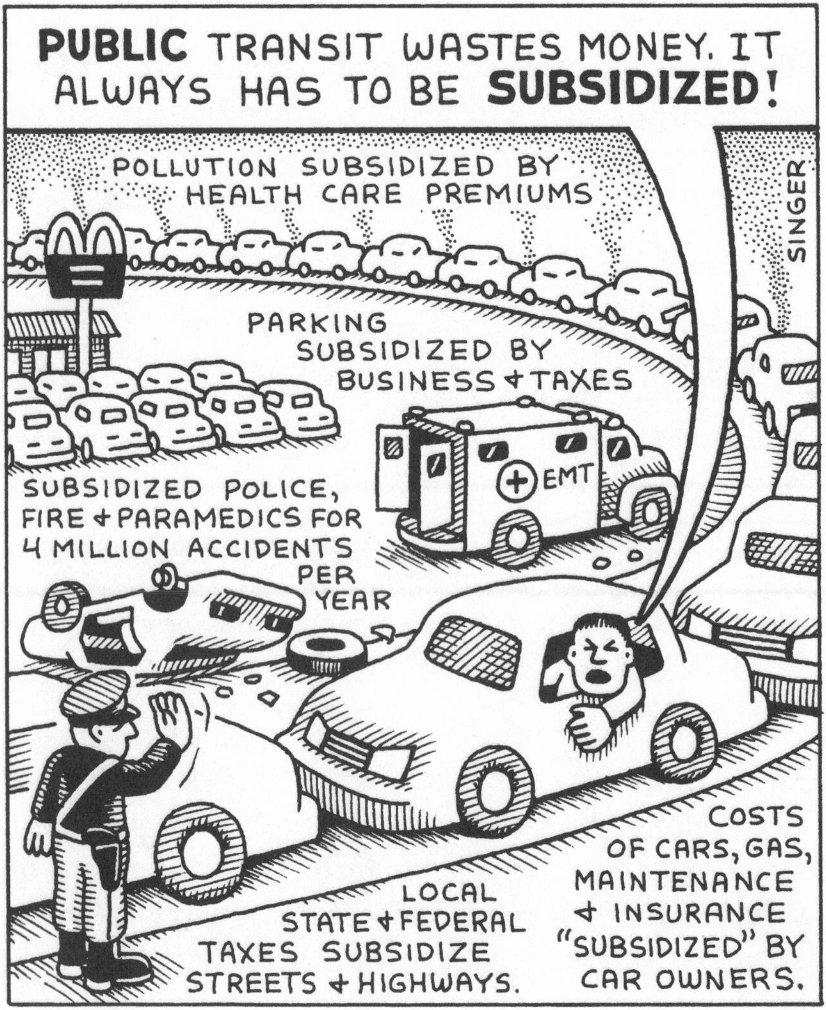
PUBLIC TRANSIT WASTES MONEY. IT ALWAYS HAS TO BE SUBSIDIZED!
POLLUTION SUBSIDIZED BY HEALTH CARE PREMIUMS
SINGER
PARKING SUBSIDIZED BY BUSINESS & TAXES
EMT
SUBSIDIZED POLICE, FIRE & PARAMEDICS FOR 4 MILLION ACCIDENTS PER YEAR
LOCAL STATE & FEDERAL TAXES SUBSIDIZE STREETS & HIGHWAYS.
COSTS OF CARS, GAS, MAINTENANCE & INSURANCE "SUBSIDIZED" BY CAR OWNERS.

This loss of property tax revenue is a hidden subsidy that motor vehicles receive from our society. This cartoon shows a few of the other subsidies. These include the billions of dollars in healthcare costs and lost productivity associated with air pollution, and the costs of subsidized parking to businesses, employees, and customers. Seventy percent of all state and local law enforcement activities are expended on cars and traffic management issues. 15 percent of all fires and 16 percent of all paramedic calls are related to cars.[16]

Then there are the costs of the highways and cars themselves and the costs of the 5.4 million U.S. highway accidents and 33,000 deaths each year.[17] Lastly, there are the so-called "external" costs of maintaining armies and carrier battle groups in the Persian Gulf, and the costs of global warming, water pollution, and a host of other environmental problems.

16   Outdoor Air Quality, American Lung Association, 2013, at http://www.lung.org/associations/charters/mid-atlantic/air-quality/outdoor-air-quality.html
Jane Holtz Kay, *Asphalt Nation* (Berkeley: University of California Press, 1997), pgs. 124, 126

17   National Highway Safety Administration, Traffic Safety Facts, 2010 Motor Vehicle Crashes: Overview, Revised February 2012, http://www-nrd.nhtsa.dot.gov/Pubs/811552.pdf

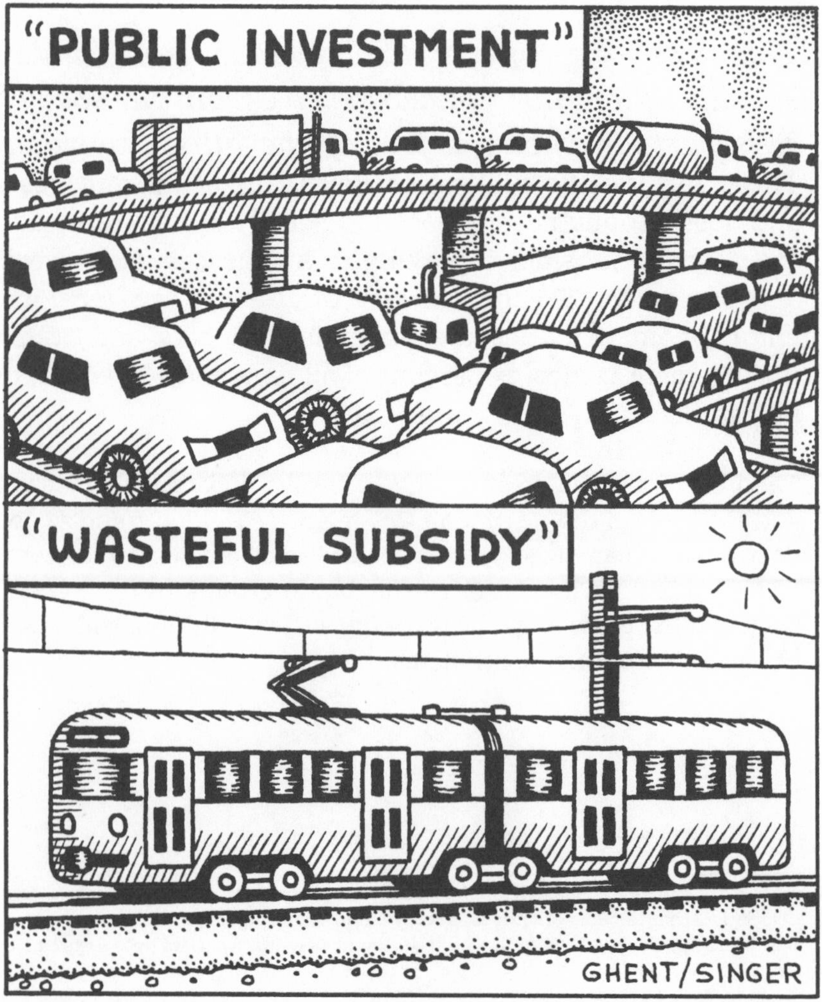
"PUBLIC INVESTMENT"
"WASTEFUL SUBSIDY"
GHENT/SINGER

With the help of groups like the Minnesota Tax Payers League, cars have managed to completely twist language and public thinking. Gas taxes and user fees pay just 51 percent of highway costs. The remaining 49 percent is paid out of general tax revenues like sales taxes, property taxes, or other non-vehicle sources. Many of the taxpayers paying for these highways don't even own cars.[18]

---

18   Joseph Henchman, The Tax Foundation, January 17, 2013, http://taxfoundation. org/blog/road-spending-state-funded-user-taxes-and-fees-including-federal-gas-tax-revenues

"Analysis Finds Shifting Trends in Highway Funding: User Fees Make up Decreasing Share," Subsidy Scope, Initiative of the Pew Charitable Foundation, updated November 25, 2009, http://subsidyscope.org/transportation/direct-expenditures/highways/funding/analysis/

WHO WILL DRIVE MORE CAREFULLY?

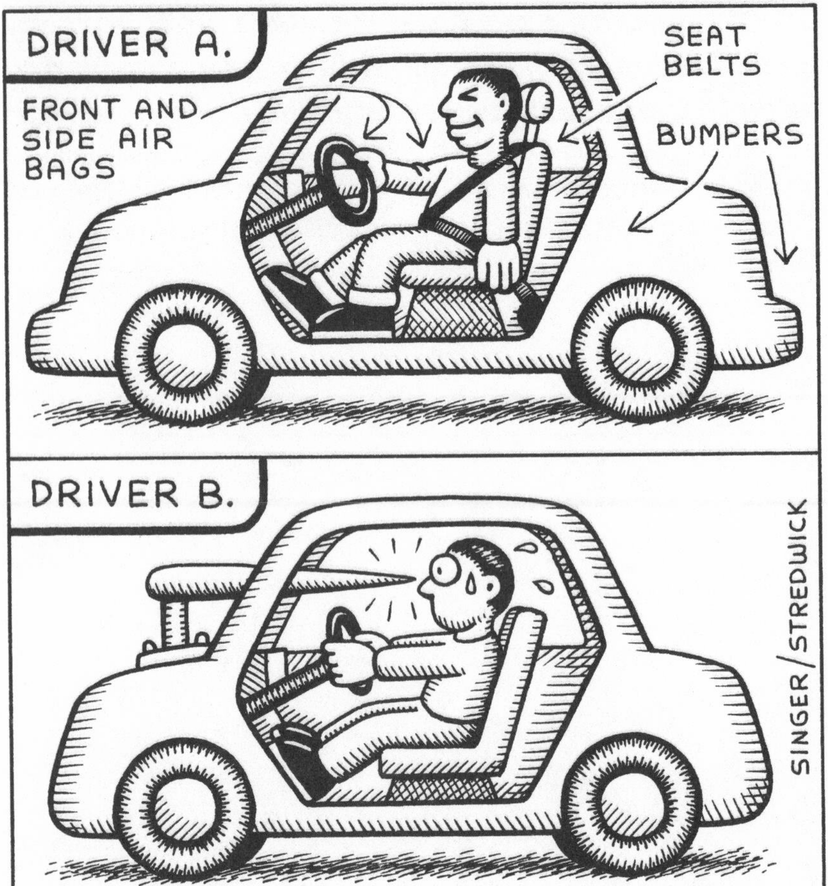
DRIVER A.
FRONT AND SIDE AIR BAGS
SEAT BELTS
BUMPERS
DRIVER B.
SINGER/STREDWICK

Automobile advocates have even twisted around the notion of "safety." They'll argue for widening or straightening a road to increase safety, but safety for whom? Certainly not for pedestrians. Each year in the U.S, cars kill 5,000 pedestrians and cyclists, and seriously injure over 100,000.[19] In developing countries, cars have surpassed most diseases to become one of the leading killers of human beings, especially children. By killing and maiming us, cars take away our public space. We put safety devices in cars to protect drivers, but do little to protect pedestrians, cyclists, and people outside of cars. Maybe if driving was more dangerous for drivers, they would slow down and drive more carefully.

---

19   Bicyclinginfo.org and Walkinginfo.org (looking at statistics for the past decade).

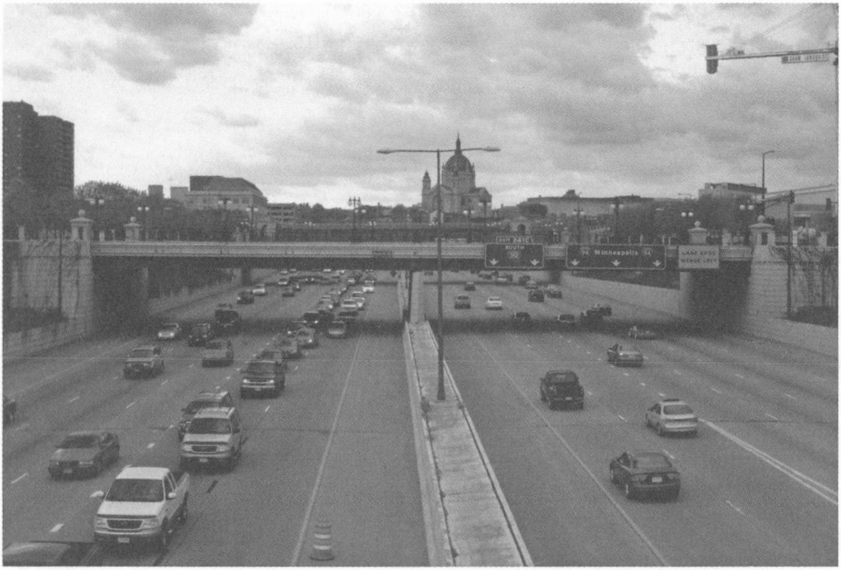
Minneapolis

In the typical American city, money is made in downtown on weekdays. It is then whisked out to outlying neighborhoods and suburbs on the freeways that isolate downtown from the rest of the city. The big concrete trenches of Interstates 94 and 35 pin downtown St. Paul, Minnesota against the river and isolate it from its neighborhoods. This is why so few people come downtown on nights and weekends.

I'm sure you can find highways in your own city that have a similar isolating effect on a neighborhood or downtown area.

In addition to destroying urban areas, the car's need for space produces sprawl, creating spread out, man-made spaces that can only be negotiated by car.

These before and after drawings contrast the kinds of development and land use that accompany railways versus highways.

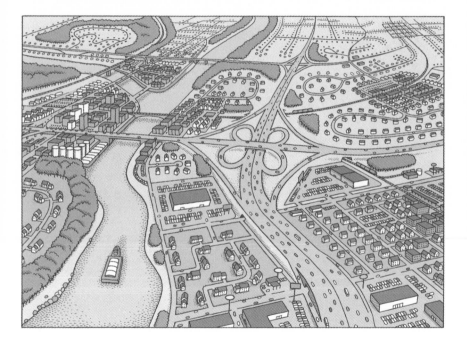

In sprawling suburbs and exurbs, young people, the elderly, and anyone else who is unable to drive finds themselves trapped in their homes, dependent on drivers to be carted to social events, schools, and essential services.

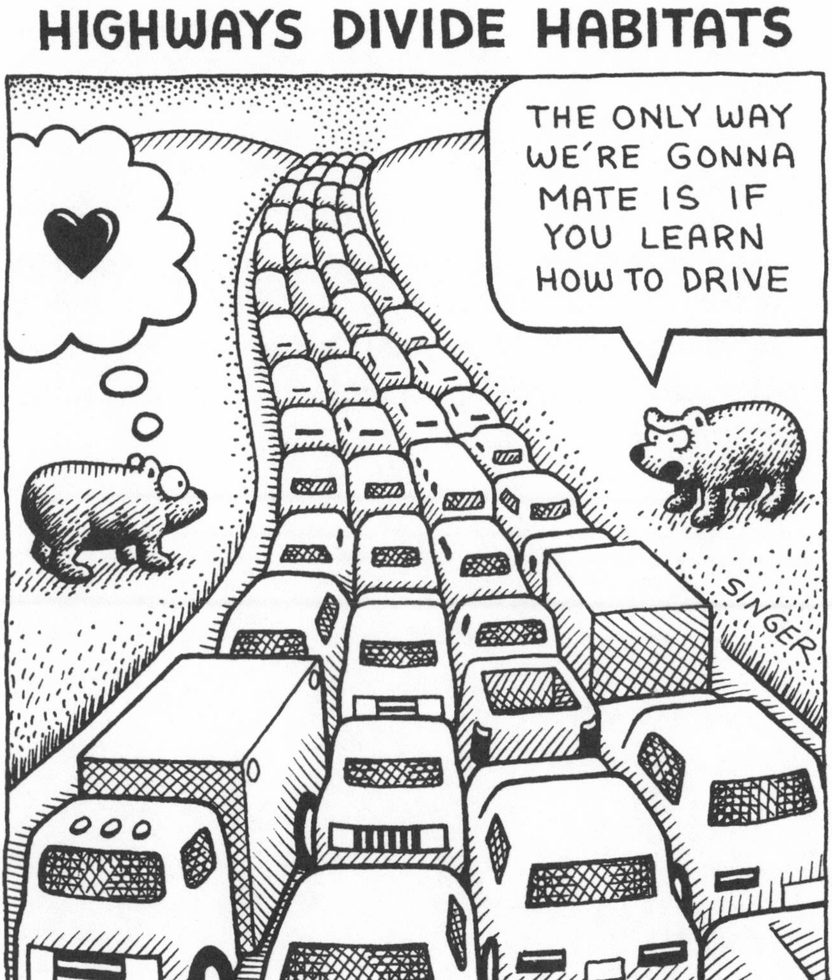
HIGHWAYS DIVIDE HABITATS
THE ONLY WAY WE'RE GONNA MATE IS IF YOU LEARN HOW TO DRIVE
SINGER

Sprawl and highways divide habitats. Each year, cars kill hundreds of millions of animals in the U.S. alone and genetically isolate the ones that survive. They are a major threat to many endangered species, including caribou, Florida panthers, and China's giant pandas.[20]

---

20   Matthew Braunstein, "Driving Animals to Their Graves," *Auto Free Times* (Arcata, CA, Fossil Fuels Policy Action Institute), Spring 1996, pp 12-13. (Figure based on Humane Society studies in the 1950s and 1970s, showing a million animals die each day on U.S. roads, including mammals, birds, reptiles, and amphibians.)
...And Chris Catton, *Pandas* (New York, Facts on File Publications, 1990), pp 118-119. Cf: *National Geographic Society*, Secrets of the Wild Panda, 1994, video.

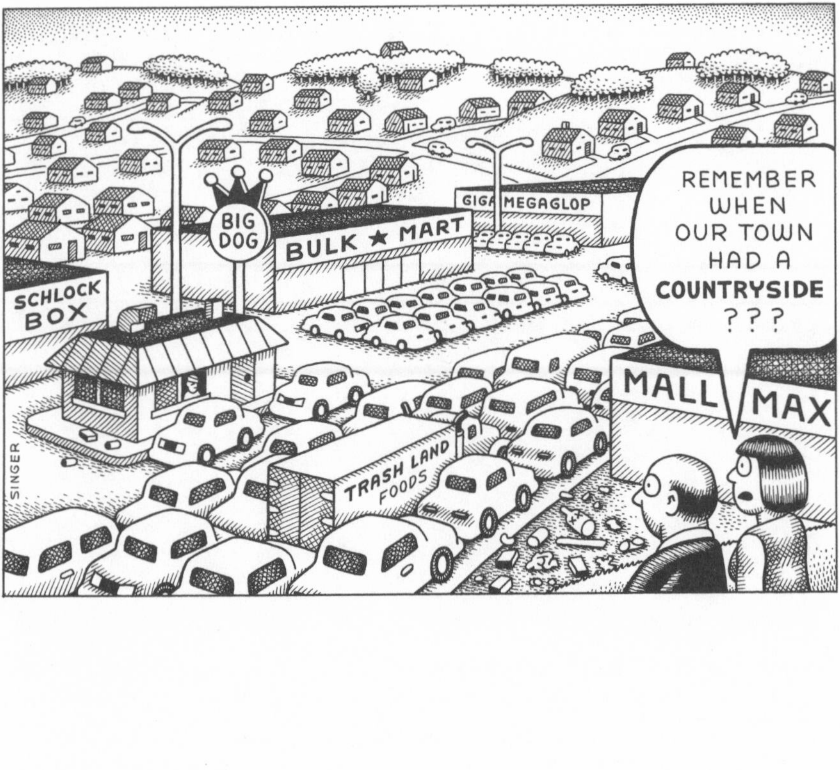
GIGA MEGAGLOP
BIG DOG
BULK ★ MART
SCHLOCK BOX
TRASH LAND FOODS
MALL MAX
REMEMBER WHEN OUR TOWN HAD A COUNTRYSIDE ???
SINGER

Most of all, sprawl is bad precisely because it is inefficient. It requires more fuel, land, resources, and time to transport people to and from employment and essential services.

In general, the farther apart people live, the more time, land, and energy is required to transport them.

This destroys green space...

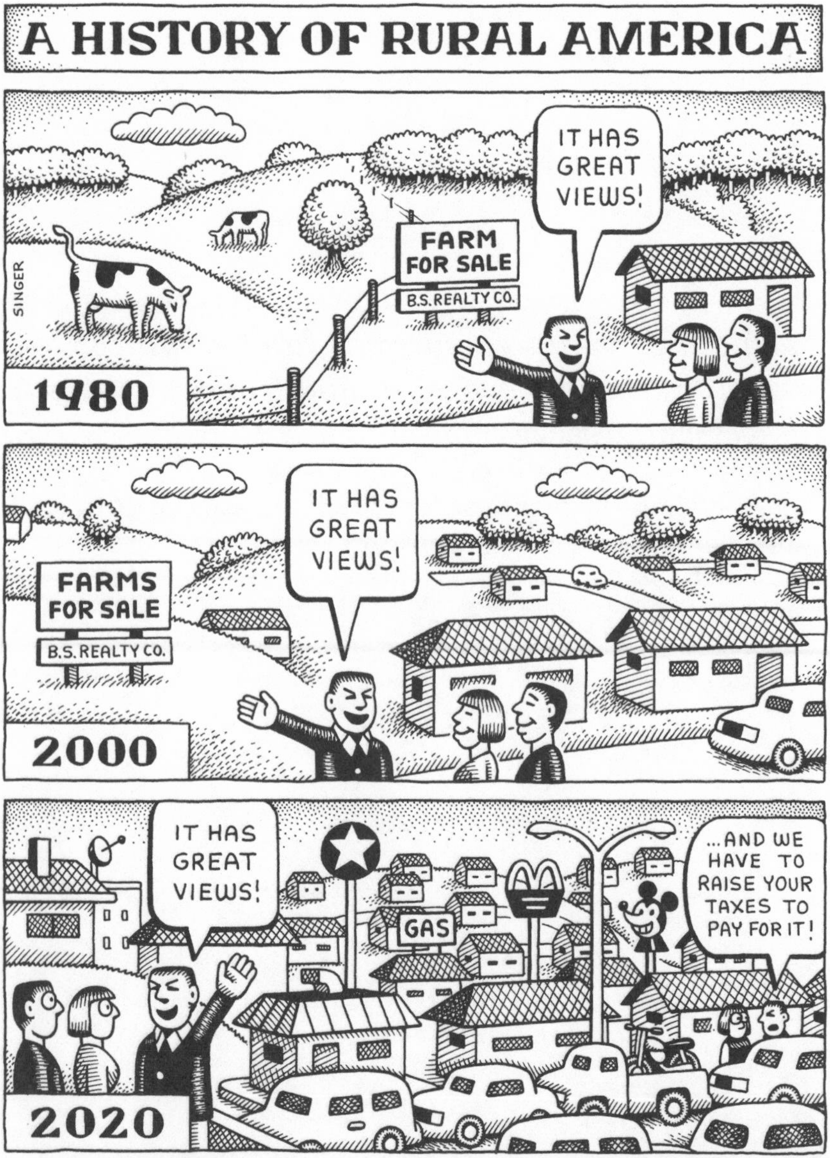
A HISTORY OF RURAL AMERICA
SINGER
FARM FOR SALE
B.S. REALTY CO.
IT HAS GREAT VIEWS!
1980
FARMS FOR SALE
B.S. REALTY CO.
IT HAS GREAT VIEWS!
2000
IT HAS GREAT VIEWS!
GAS
...AND WE HAVE TO RAISE YOUR TAXES TO PAY FOR IT!
2020

...and it destroys farmland. According to the Leopold Institute at Iowa State University, the average bite of food now travels 1,500 miles to reach your dinner plate. Because of sprawl and the lack of farms around American cities, we have become dependent on petroleum just to eat! When oil prices go up, the price of food and other commodities can thus rise sharply as well, leading to major inflation. Because food and goods are traveling much farther, this pending bout of inflation could be much worse than it was in the 1970s.[21]

---

21   *Rich Pirog, "Checking the food odometer: Comparing food miles for local versus conventional produce sales to Iowa institutions," (Ames, Iowa, Leopold Center for Sustainable Agriculture, Iowa State University, 2003), http://www.leopold.iastate.edu/sites/default/files/pubs-and-papers/2003-07-checking-food-odometer-comparing-food-miles-local-versus-conventional-produce-sales-iowa-institution.pdf*

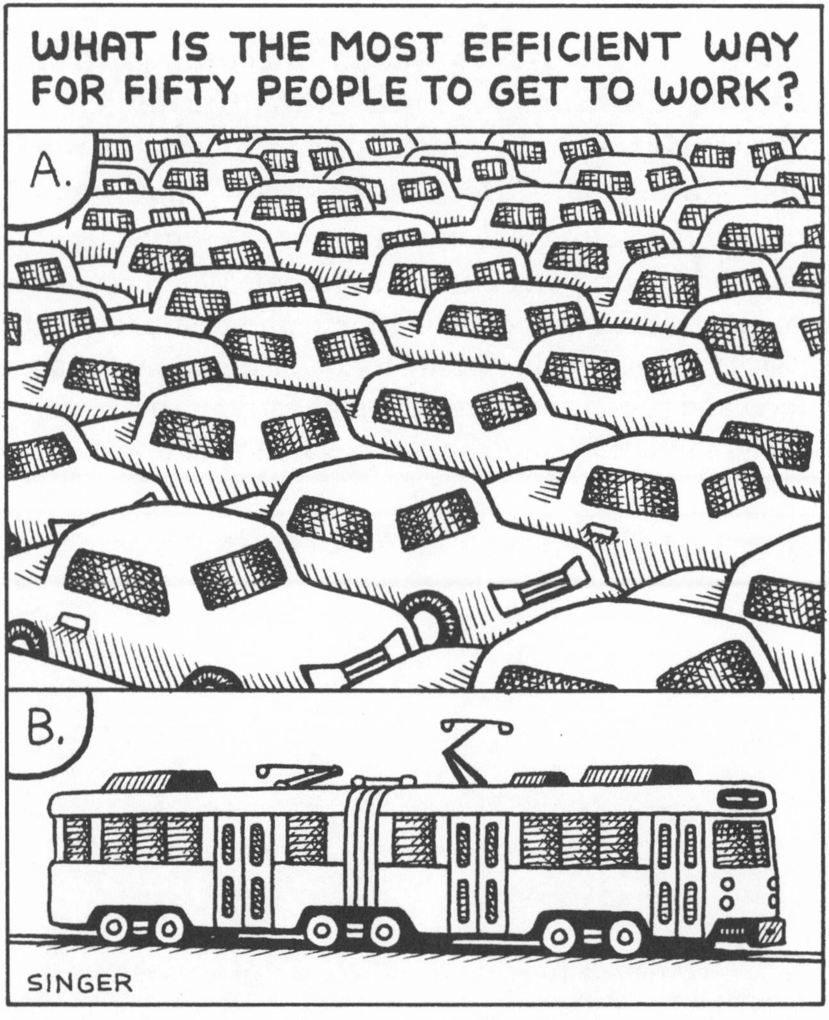
WHAT IS THE MOST EFFICIENT WAY FOR FIFTY PEOPLE TO GET TO WORK?
A.
B.
SINGER

Freeways are an inefficient way to move people. A highway lane can move just 1,500 cars per hour. Even if everyone rode in 3-person carpools, this would mean the highway lane could only move 4,500 people per hour. This compares to nearly 40,000 people per hour that can be moved on a single track of transit, or over 50,000 people per hour, per lane, if they all walked or rode bicycles.[22]

Now this deserves a little explanation. If you've ever taken a driver's education class, you're taught to keep a two-second following distance from the car in front of you. This turns out to be about the distance people actually keep in peak traffic. Thus, with two seconds between cars, a typical highway lane can accommodate 30 cars per minute or 1,800 cars per hour. Because people are entering, exiting, and changing lanes, however, capacity is reduced and the accepted engineering standard is about 1,500 cars per hour, per lane.

Now think of a single track of transit, which has about the same spatial displacement as a highway lane. A typical 10-car subway train holds nearly 2,000 people. If you operate trains at 5-minute headways, you can fit twelve trains per hour on that track and move 24,000 people per hour. If you operate trains more frequently or use split-level commuter train cars, you can double that capacity to nearly 40,000 people per hour.

So transit's biggest advantage over cars is capacity. The automobile by its very nature is an inefficient people mover, and this inefficiency and need for space means that it creates sprawl.

---

22   Robert A. Caro, *The Power Broker*, (New York, Vintage Books, 1974), p. 901, 945.

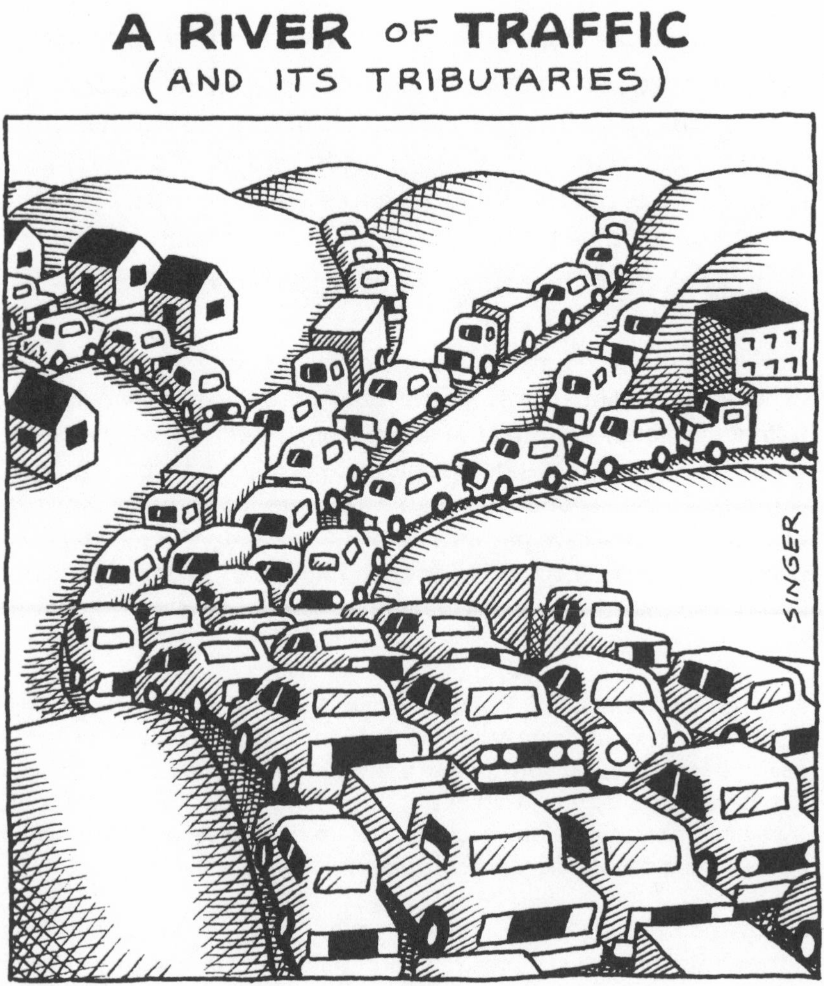
A RIVER OF TRAFFIC
(AND ITS TRIBUTARIES)
SINGER

Nevertheless, when confronted with traffic congestion, transportation departments continue to build more lanes and more highways. Yet, in a hundred years of history, adding new lanes and highways have only generated more traffic. Engineers now call this phenomenon "Traffic Generation." Economists call it "induced demand." More roads merely encourage people to move farther away from downtowns, encourage more sprawl and more unnecessary car trips at peak hours.[23]

23   Thomas Bass, "Road to Ruin," *Discover*, May 1992, pg. 56-61. Cf: Arnott Richard and Kenneth Small, "the economics of Traffic congestion" *American Scientist* (North Carolina Scientific Research Society), volume 82. Sept.-Oct. 1994, pp. 446-455; Anthony Downs, *Stuck in Traffic,* (Washington DC, Brookings Institution, 1992) pp. 26-34; Todd Litman, "Generated Traffic—Implications for Transport Planning," Victoria Transport Policy Institute, 1999, http://www.vtpi.org/gentraf.pdf

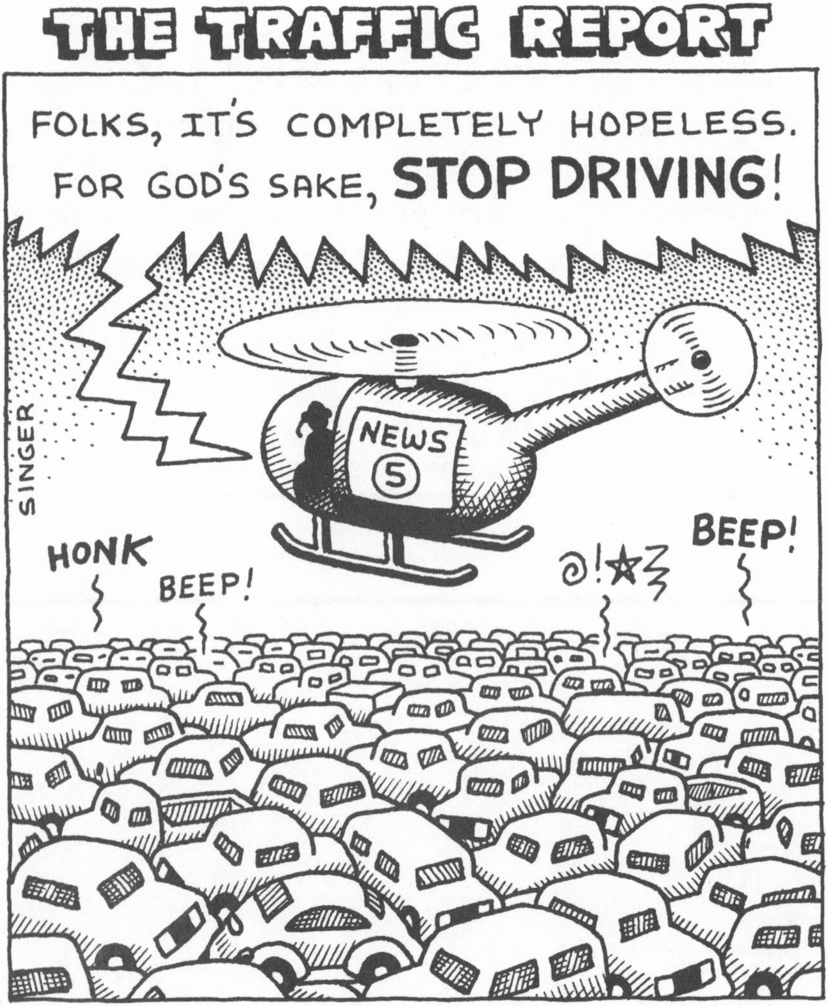
THE TRAFFIC REPORT
FOLKS, IT'S COMPLETELY HOPELESS. FOR GOD'S SAKE, STOP DRIVING!
NEWS 5
SINGER
HONK
BEEP!
@!★Z
BEEP!

How have we gotten to this point? Given all the drawbacks of cars, why do we still build highways? Why don't we spend more money on transit, or on creating denser, car-free cities? What forces drive the spread of highways and how can we stop them? To answer these questions we need to look at American history.

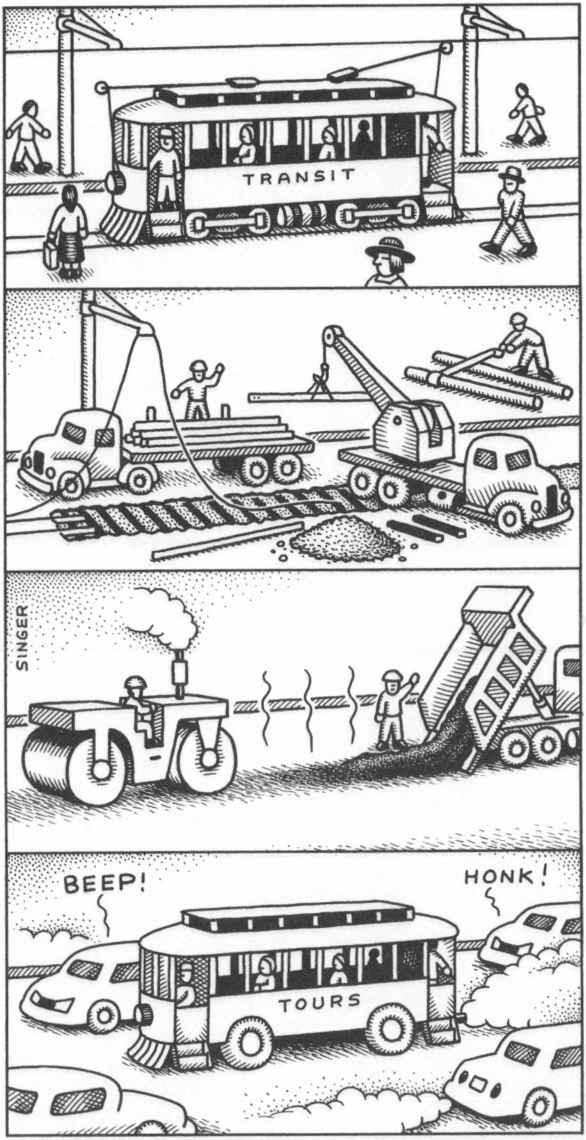
TRANSIT
SINGER
BEEP!
HONK!
TOURS

By the late 1920s, most Americans lived in cities. The automobile was just starting to take hold. Car makers had glutted the market for cars, primarily by selling them to suburbanites and rural folks. If automobile manufacturers wanted to expand the market for cars, they needed to sell them to people in cities. In 1923, General Motors president Alfred Sloan said, "[the leveling of demand for new cars] means a change from easy selling to hard selling ...[it is necessary to] reorder society, ...to alter the environment in which automobiles are sold."[24]

Since people in cities had great public transit and interurban rail systems, GM and other auto makers decided that they needed to eliminate these systems or convert them to buses, thus inducing more urbanites to buy cars. GM began building buses as early as 1925 and formed and owned a controlling interest in Greyhound. GM then joined forces with Standard Oil of California, Firestone, Mac Truck, and Philips Petroleum to form and finance a front company—National City Lines—whose job was to buy up urban rail networks and convert them to buses. Aided by the depression and the "Public Utilities Holding Company Act" of 1935, National City Lines was able to buy up and dismantle over 100 rail transit systems in over 45 U.S. cities.

In 1949 GM and its partners were convicted of conspiracy, a conviction that was upheld by a federal appeals court in 1951.[25] Unfortunately, the punishment for destroying America's transit systems was a slap on the wrist. Each company got a five thousand dollar fine. No one went to jail, and the companies pocketed billions of dollars from the increased sales of cars and buses.

24   Stephen Goddard, *Getting There: The Epic Struggle Between Road and Rail in the American Century,* (New York: Basic Books, 1994), pg. 125-126
25   United States v. National City Lines, 186 F.2d 561, C.A.7 (Ill.), 1951

This is one of my favorite pictures of that era because it depicts politics at its sleaziest. It was taken in Saint Paul, Minnesota, in 1954. The man on the right is Fred Ossanna. He was a former National City Lines attorney with links to organized crime. In 1949, he was put in charge of Twin Cities Rapid Transit company (TCRT). The Twin Cities had an extensive public transit system with 530 miles of track and over 700 transit cars, many of which were built right in Minneapolis. Ossanna brought in General Motors as a consultant, who helped him to finance the conversion of Twin Cities Rapid Transit to GM buses. Ossanna ripped up the tracks, sold off some of the trolleys to Mexico and burned the rest. Here he is receiving a check for his handiwork from TCRT vice-president James Towey as the last of the trolley cars burn. Six years later, both men would be convicted of fraud, conspiracy, and embezzlement.[26]

While there were other factors that contributed to the destruction of public transit, auto and oil industry greed for increased sales and profits were major factors. Having done this, the auto manufacturers needed more roads and highways for their cars. In 1920s and 1930s America, building roads across county and state lines was legally and practically very difficult. So car makers and the car clubs they created (like AAA) turned to state and federal governments.

---

26   United States Court of Appeals Eight Circuit, Isaacs v. United States, 301 F.2d 706 (1962).
Photo courtesy of the Minneapolis Public Library, Minneapolis Collection.

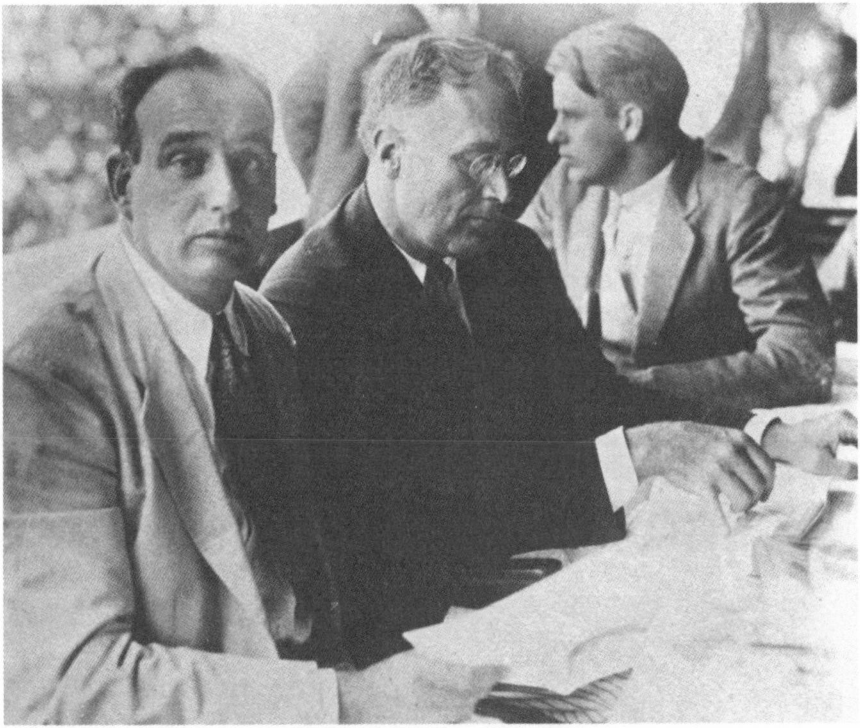

In this 1920s photograph, the man on the left is Robert Moses, then a little known government bureaucrat in New York State. Beginning in 1920, Moses helped successive New York governors to streamline state government and helped create modern government "agencies." He was also the first to create the modern highway department or "authority." In the early days, the preferred way to finance roads and bridges was with tolls. Authorities were government sanctioned corporations that borrowed money by issuing bonds to pay for the construction of a particular road or bridge. The bonds would be paid off by charging tolls. Since drivers flocked to the new roads and bridges in record numbers, banks quickly realized that toll roads were a great investment and were willing to lend Moses and other state highway agencies huge sums of money based on projected toll revenues. All this money built yet more roads. More importantly, this money represented tens of thousands of jobs for unions, engineering firms, construction firms, lawyers, and public relations firms.

The ability to hire all these employees, gave Moses and other agency heads incredible political power. The highway agencies were no longer beholden to politicians to give them money. Quite the opposite, their control over toll revenues gave them power over the politicians and enabled them to extort even more money out of state legislatures.

One man who learned this from Moses was Franklin Delano Roosevelt. He's seen here, sitting to the right of Moses, when he was governor of New York. When Roosevelt became president in 1932, he borrowed many of Moses' ideas and created federal agencies like the WPA and the Bureau of Reclamation, to help revive the U.S. economy. He also borrowed Moses' love of the automobile and many of the WPA's projects were highways and bridges for cars.

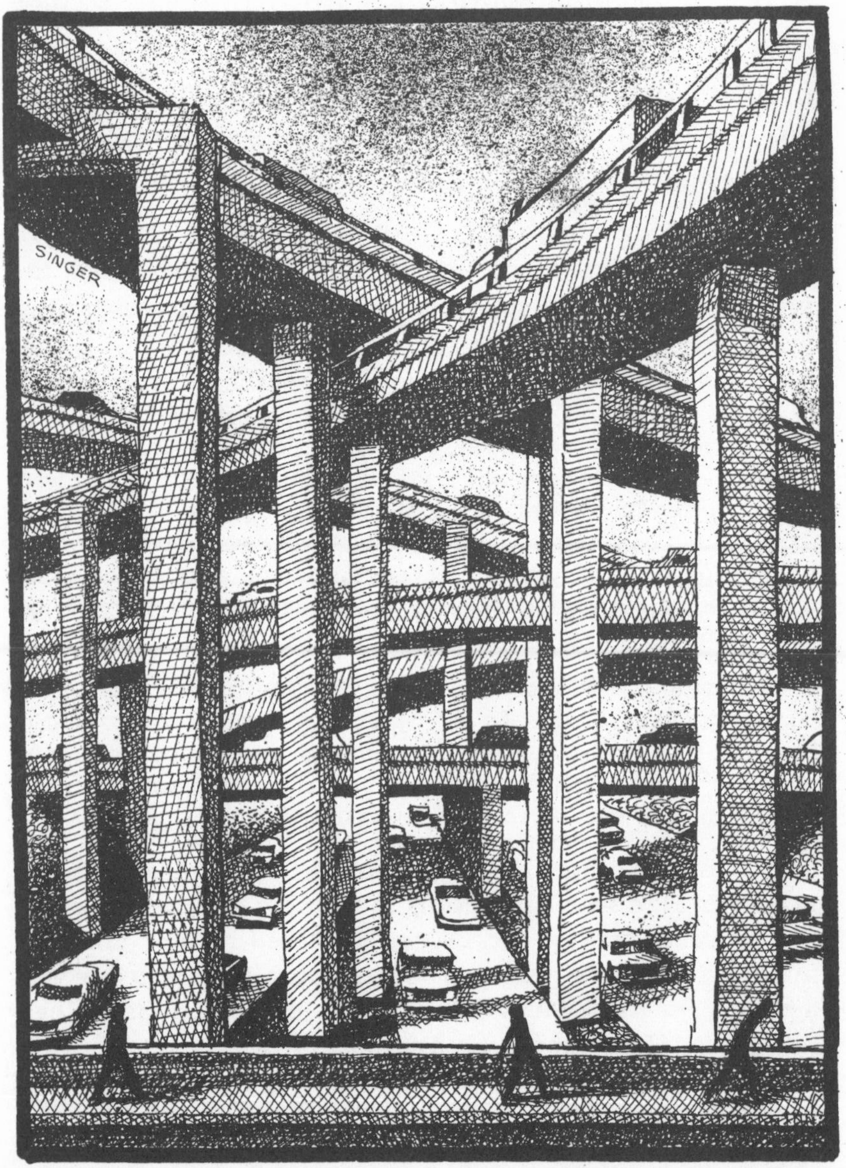
SINGER

Prior to Moses and Roosevelt, political power lay strictly in the hands of the wealthy and in physical communities. If a party boss wanted to be re-elected, he had to give jobs, money, and graft back to the community in which he lived.

In the new system—the agency system—political power lay in broader groups. These included unions, professional trade associations, and interest groups associated with a particular agency. All of these groups crossed physical community boundaries and thus political power ceased to be community based. A party boss could now put a freeway through part of his neighborhood, or destroy it entirely and still be re-elected. In the new system, government agency chiefs and the agencies themselves wielded ultimate political power. Politicians came and went, but the chiefs and the agencies remained. Sometimes the politicians could control the agencies and sometimes they couldn't. Term limits for elected officials in many states have only made this problem worse.

To this day, much of what happens in politics is agency driven. You have intelligence agencies, defense agencies, energy departments, state university systems, housing authorities, space agencies, each with their own constituent base. Defense agencies have created a "military industrial complex." The Bureau of Reclamation and its dams and canals have created a vast web of interests around irrigation and water policy. And highways have created what I like to call "the highway industrial complex."

One reason why Roosevelt, states, and cities chose to pump public money into highways rather than railways and public transit was that, in 1930s America, all of the railways and public transit systems were privately owned and relatively profitable. So it didn't make much sense to subsidize them.

In Europe, by contrast, most of the railways and public transit systems had been battered by World War I and either received public financing or had been nationalized. Thus, european railway and transit agencies predated their highway cousins and could easily compete with them for public funding. After World War II, Europe poured a lot of its Marshall Plan money and government subsidies into rebuilding their railways and urban transit systems, even as the United States was pouring its money into building interstate highways. This is the reason why, to this day, Europe's rail and transit systems are vastly superior to those in America and the reason that Europe is a more urban society.[27]

The U.S. didn't create public transit agencies and national railways (like Amtrak and Conrail) until the 1960s and 70s, when private railroads and transit companies started going bankrupt. U.S. railway and transit companies went bankrupt precisely because they were forced to compete with an ever-growing, largely free system of publicly subsidized highways.

---

27   Photo by Joost J. Bakker Ijmuiden, licensed under the Creative Commons Attribution 2.0 Generic License, as posted at: http://commons.wikimedia.org/wiki/File:TGV_Train_à_Grande_Vitesse.jpg

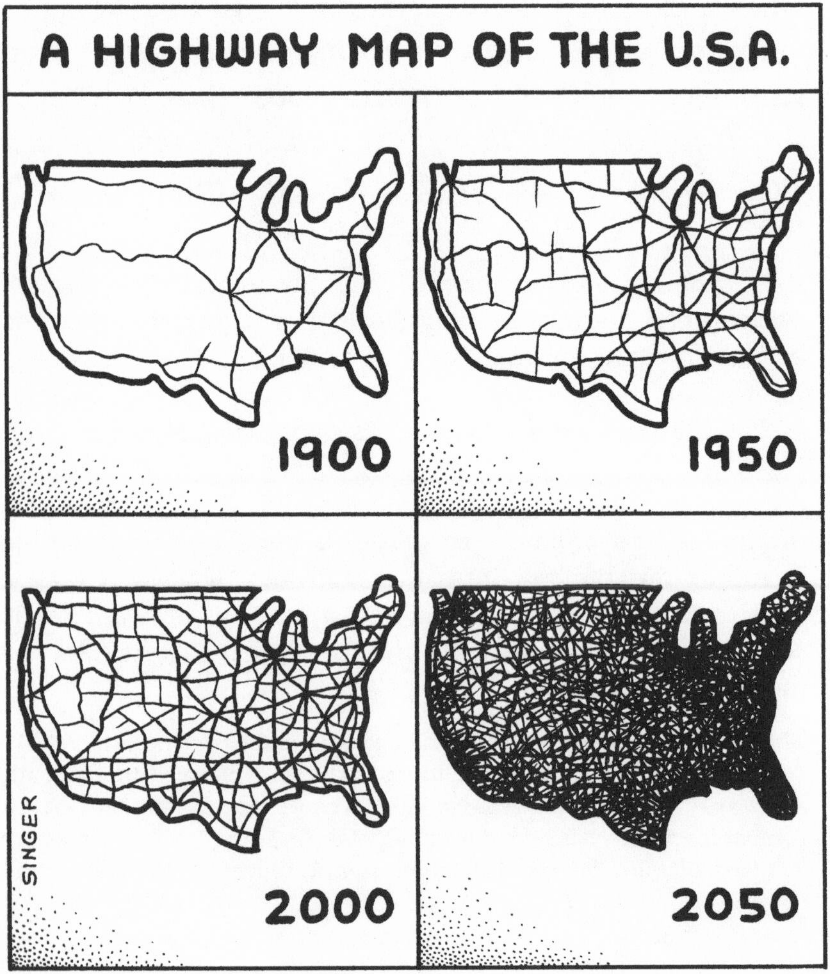
A HIGHWAY MAP OF THE U.S.A.
1900
1950
2000
2050
SINGER

The nature of agencies is that they try to grow larger and more powerful, in order to get more money and jobs for themselves. Agencies that have external sources of revenue, outside of legislatures, have more political power. State university control of tuition dollars and private research grants are an example of this. Agencies that don't have external sources of revenue have less power, like certain welfare agencies that are entirely dependant on the legislature for their budget.

By the mid 1950s, highway agencies had managed to get exclusive control of billions of dollars in federal and state gas taxes. In this way, they became the most powerful political force in state politics. Politicians who challenged a highway agency were quickly ejected from office. Engineers or public officials who crossed them often had their careers ruined.

This basic paradigm of revenue control and agency politics is the reason that America has built and continues to build so many roads. It's why little or no money goes to transit and why the number of cars, oil consumption, and sprawl continues to grow. It's also a major reason why we spend billions of dollars on new bridges, highways, and lane expansions, even as our old bridges and highways fall apart.[28]

---

28   Curtis Tate and Greg Gordon, "U.S. keeps building new highways while letting old ones crumble," *McClatchy Newspapers*, February 3, 2013, http://www.mcclatchydc.com/2013/02/03/181506/us-keeps-building-new-highways.html#.UYoSiK7X-so

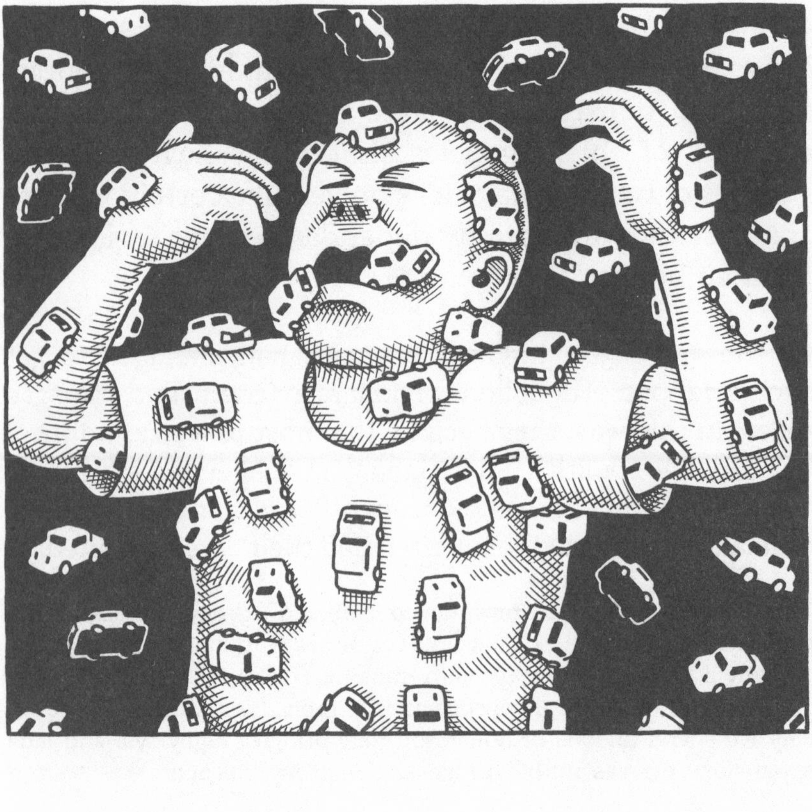

The Minnesota Department of Transportation can spend over a billion dollars a year, much of which doesn't even pass through the legislature but comes directly to the agency from state and federal gas taxes. MnDOT's control over this money gives them incredible political power. The agency literally owns legislators—people like Mark Ourada, a former Republican state senator whose private road-building employer received 74 million dollars in MnDOT contracts. To quote Kent Allin:

> "The culture of MnDOT is to act the bully, throw one's weight around and villanize anybody who stands in your way and not worry about wasting tax dollars. ...MnDOT ...is trying to bully us into giving them exactly what they want, regardless of whether it is lawful or responsible to do so. I believe we have been pushed to a point where we either assert our oversight role ...or tacitly admit that we are totally ineffectual in that role with respect to MnDOT."

Kent Allin was a 21-year state auditor who was fired in 2002 for speaking out against no-bid MnDOT highway contracts.[29]

This same sort of thing happens in other states and there are many stories suggesting that other DOTs also use their political might to bully opponents into submission, either directly or through local Metropolitan Planning Organizations. Many highway agencies, like the Pennsylvania Turnpike Authority, spend a million dollars per year just lobbying state and federal law makers. Others are able to influence politicians by paying them legal "retainer" fees or via contracts to their employers.

---

29   Pat Doyle; Dan Browning, "MnDOT contracts called illegal; State watchdog fired shortly after his harsh criticisms surface," *Minneapolis Star Tribune*, March 15, 2002, Pg 1A.

ARROGANT PATERNALISM

OR "TRUST US, WE'RE SMARTER THAN YOU ARE"

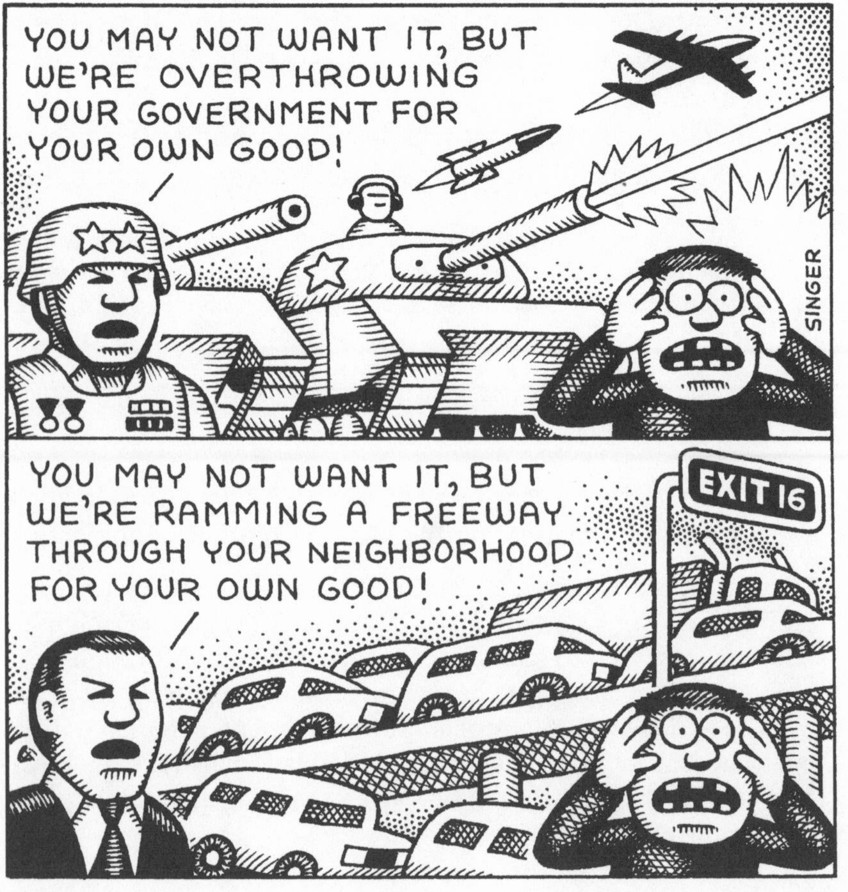
YOU MAY NOT WANT IT, BUT WE'RE OVERTHROWING YOUR GOVERNMENT FOR YOUR OWN GOOD!
SINGER
YOU MAY NOT WANT IT, BUT WE'RE RAMMING A FREEWAY THROUGH YOUR NEIGHBORHOOD FOR YOUR OWN GOOD!
EXIT 16

To ensure its power, MnDOT has a provision in the state constitiution mandating that state gas tax dollars have to be spent on highways. This is typical of most U.S. states. These constitutional amendments were passed between 1930 and the mid 1950s due to lobbying by oil and car companies and in response to the federal Hayden Cartwright Act of 1936. The act required states to "dedicate" their fuel taxes to highways or lose federal road funding. Some states, like Alabama, have constitutional amendments that actually forbid the state from funding public transit at all. This is why the city of Montgomery has just 12 bus lines that stop running at 9pm on weekdays, 6pm on Saturdays and don't run at all on Sundays.[30]

In order to stop sprawl and get more money for public transit, highway agences must be prevented from building new roads. There are two strategies for doing this. The first is to amend state constitutions to allow gas tax money to be spent on transit, other non-automotive transportation modes, and better land use. This is what some refer to as "flexing" gas taxes or toll revenues. The second strategy is through "road pricing"—the use of taxes and tolls to try and reduce demand. On the surface, this second strategy sounds logical—increase driving costs and people will drive less. But the key is who gets these new tax and toll revenues. Right now only the highway agencies receive this money and they spend it to build more highways.

---

30   Debbie Elliott, Montgomery Transit System in Poor Shape, *All Things Considered,* National Public Radio, December 3, 2005, http://www.npr.org/templates/story/story.php?storyId=5038225, cf. Amendment 93, http://arisecitizens.org/index.php/publications-topmenu-32/fact-sheets-topmenu-36/public-transportation-topmenu-60/1587-public-transportation-policy-choices-2012

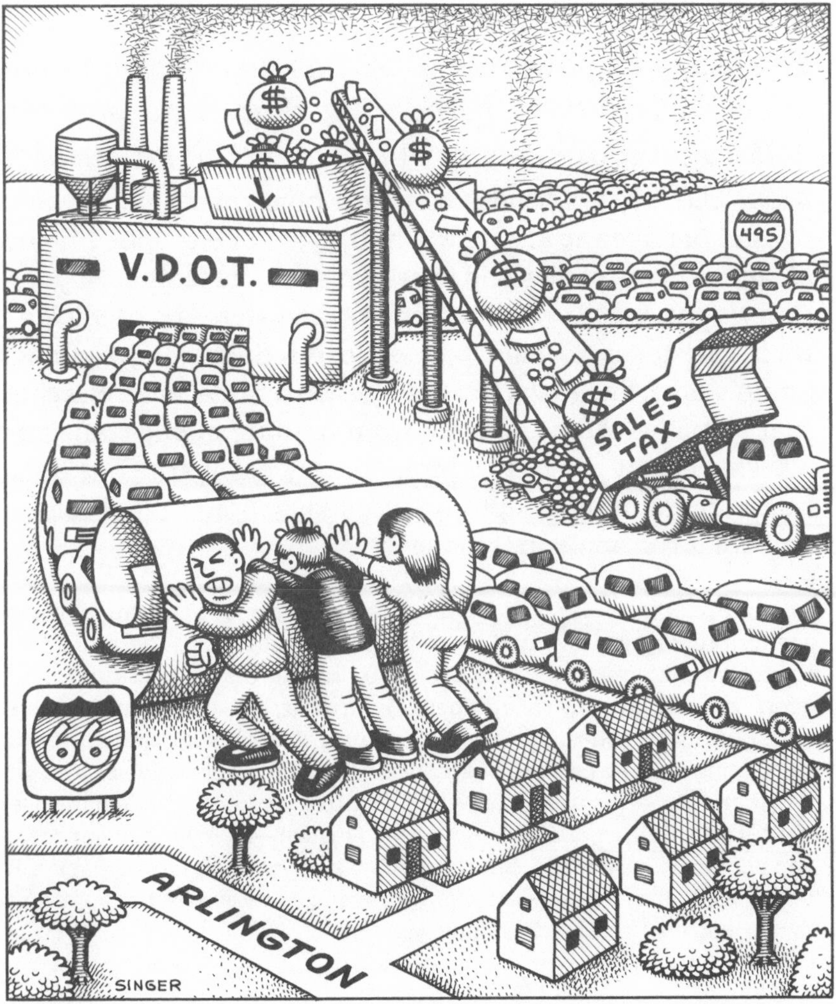
V.D.O.T.
$
495
SALES TAX
66
ARLINGTON
SINGER

Highway agencies have always used their financial and political clout to squeeze more money out of state legislatures, either in bonding bills or as outright appropriations. When the economic downturn hit in 2001, states began to run huge deficits. Suddenly there was no more money to squeeze. To make matters worse, more fuel efficient cars started to reduce gas tax revenues. In desperation, highway agencies began turning to other schemes to generate new revenues for highway construction. For example, the Virginia DOT attempted to pass a sales tax to finance widening a beltway around the Washington, DC metro area. Using a massive grassroots campaign, anti-highway activists were able to defeat the referendum on the ballots of the affected counties. This is a poster from that campaign.

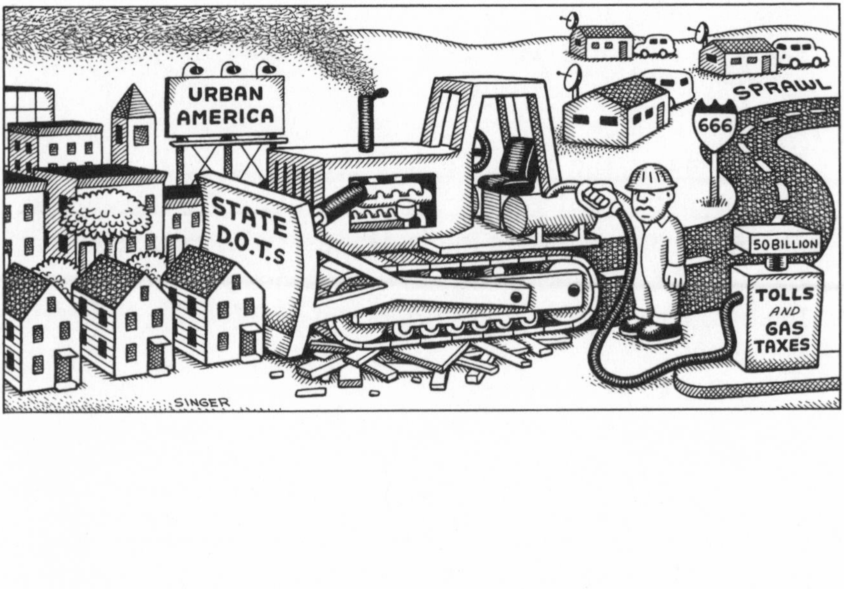
URBAN
AMERICA
STATE
D.O.T.s
SPRAWL
666
50 BILLION
TOLLS
AND
GAS
TAXES
SINGER

Highway agencies finally settled on another scheme—bringing back toll roads in what they refer to as "Fast Lane tolls." In this scheme, DOTs issue bonds to finance the construction of special "fast lanes." Commuters who want to use them pay a toll, which goes to paying off the bonds. Highway advocates sold fast lane tolling to voters by implying that it was "Road Pricing." But true Road Pricing is designed to deter people from driving at certain hours or in certain places. In contrast, fast lane tolls are merely a way to finance new highway construction. Fast lane tolling was slipped into the last six-year federal highway bill. By some estimates, it pumped over 50 billion dollars into new highway construction during the last ten years. State versions of the legislation are pending or have passed in many states, including Minnesota.[31]

Additionally, DOTs are converting High Occupancy Vehicle lanes into "Hot Lanes", allowing single occupancy drivers to use the lanes if they pay a toll, generating additional revenue for new highway projects.

Clearly, the moral of history is this: Tolls and gas taxes are useless at deterring highway construction unless the money goes directly to transit or goes into city or state general funds, where it can be controlled by politicians. If it goes back to highway agencies, more highways will be built and the agencies will only gain more political power. So, in this cartoon, you either have to cut off the money hose or redirect it to transit. A few states have done this. Pennsylvania's "Act 44" requires that a portion of its Turnpike Authority's tolls be used to subsidize transit.

Some argue that it's better if politicians control tolls and gas tax revenues rather than the highway agencies themselves. This is because politicans are elected and thus somewhat accountable to voters. By contrast, highway agency directors aren't accountable to anyone. True "road pricing" or "congestion pricing" only exists in London, Singapore, Stockholm, Milan, and a couple smaller cities, where toll revenues actually go to automobile alternatives. The devil is in the details of most legislation, and you need to look where toll revenues will go.

31   John Tierney, "Congress and White House End Taboo Against Tolls," *New York Times*, April 4, 2004, http://www.nytimes.com/2004/04/04/us/congress-and-white-house-end-taboo-against-tolls.html?n=Top%2fReference%2fTimes%20Topics%2fSubjects%2fT%2fTolls

Another way of controlling highway agencies may have been inspired by something that happened in New York City and is best represented by a piece of federal legislation called "ISTEA."

In 1970 Governor Nelson Rockefeller was able to combine Robert Moses's New York City highway Authority with New York City's transit agencies to form the Metropolitan Transportation Authority (MTA). Under the new structure, toll revenues could be used to subsidize transit and the new agency no longer had a stake in building roads. It could just as easily build transit projects, since either way it got to spend the money and grow itself.

Beginning in 1982, the federal government began setting aside a portion of gas taxes for transit. If a state DOT wanted to get this money, it had to come up with a transit project to spend it on. In 1991, Congress passed the Intermodal Surface Transportation Efficiency Act (ISTEA). For the first time, a large chunk of federal gas tax dollars could be spent "flexibly" on either roads or transit. The intent was to allow transit and non-automotive transportation to compete with highways on a level playing field. This, in turn, would give state highway agencies an incentive to diversify and become truly integrated transportation departments.

ISTEA paid for bikeways in New York (like the one depicted here) and in many other states. Its "New Starts" program paid up to 80% of the construction costs for many light rail and commuter rail systems around the country, including half of Minnesota's Hiawatha and Central Corridor light rail lines. ISTEA also produced a small shift in the culture of highway agencies because many state DOTs hired new engineers and coordinators who specialized in transit, bike, or pedestrian engineering. Often, however, these new hires were relegated to a lower status within the agency and, as always, new highways kept getting built. The states that did best tended to be the ones that already had large transit agencies or infrastructure.

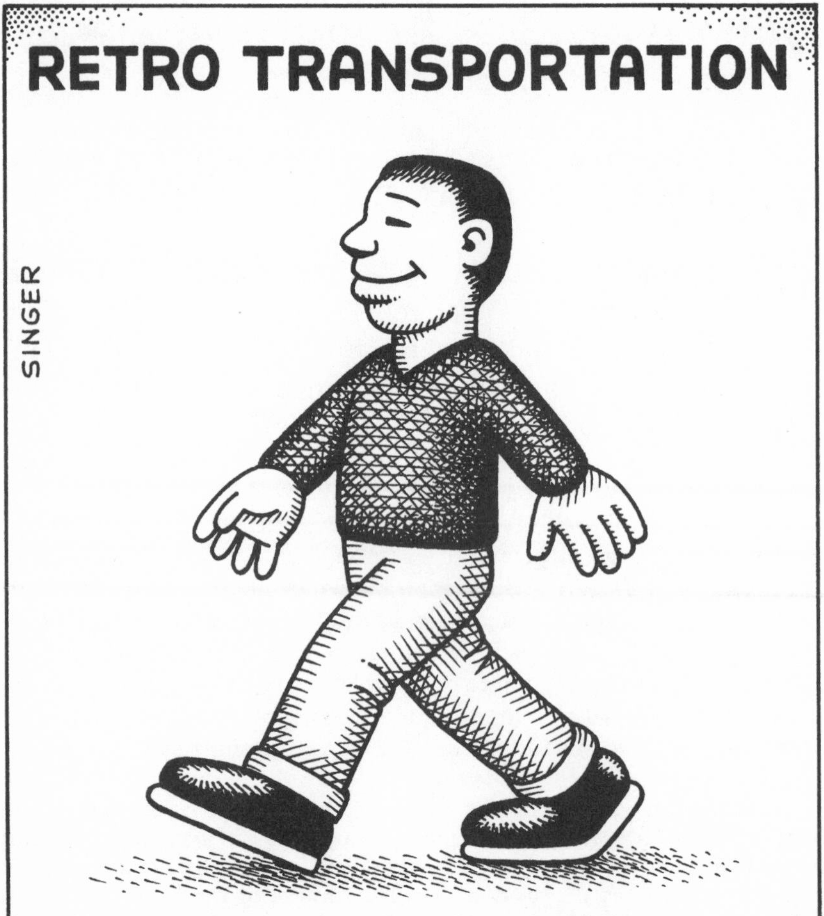
RETRO TRANSPORTATION
SINGER

This first incarnation of ISTEA allowed almost a third of all federal gas tax dollars to be used on non-automotive projects—nearly 50 billion out of a 150 billion dollar six-year budget.

Six years later, when the act was reauthorized as TEA-21, dedicated highway spending was increased to $150 billion, while flexible transit spending was kept flat. Loopholes were added that allowed off ramps and other highway-oriented peripherals to qualify as "pedestrian Improvements." Also, ISTEA left state gas tax dollars untouched, still firmly in control of the highway departments. The most recent incarnation of ISTEA enacted under the Bush administration—TEA-3 or "SAFETEA-LU"—only made this worse.

Another problem is that states are required to raise a certain percentage of local matching funds to qualify for federal transportation dollars—anywhere from 20% to 50% of the cost of a project. Because state gas taxes and motor vehicle fees are often dedicated to highways in state constitutions, it's easy for a state to come up with the necessary matching funds for a highway project. Transit projects, however, are more difficult. Unable to use state gas taxes, cities and states are forced to pay for transit with sales tax increases, business taxes, or other financing schemes. These revenue sources are more scarce, necessitate voter referendums, and put transit in competition with other non-transportation state needs. Because of this difficulty in raising state matching funds, a lot of federal dollars that could be "flexed" to transit end up being spent on roads.

To create real change, it will be necessary to to amend state constitutions and create state versions of ISTEA, allowing state gas tax and motor vehicle fee dollars to be spent on transit or non-automotive transportation. Only then will we see a substantial change in agency culture and an end of new highway construction.

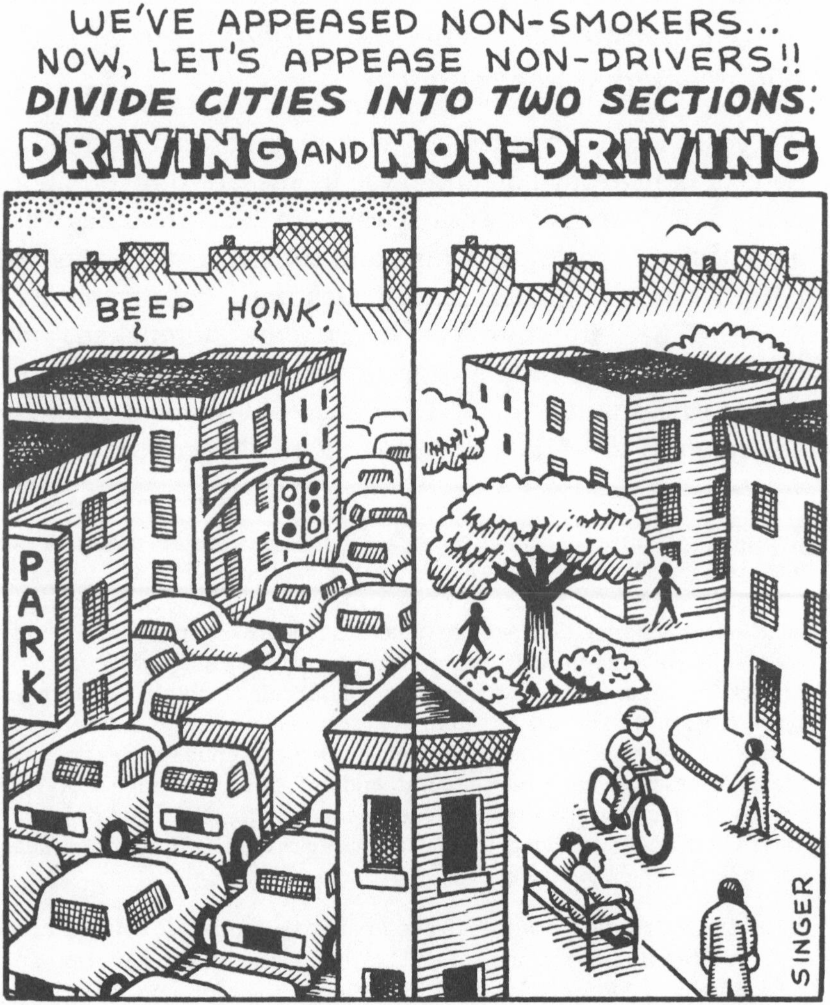
WE'VE APPEASED NON-SMOKERS...
NOW, LET'S APPEASE NON-DRIVERS!!
DIVIDE CITIES INTO TWO SECTIONS:
DRIVING AND NON-DRIVING
BEEP
HONK!
PARK
SINGER

Thus, the best way to combat highway agencies is to cut off their money supply and integrate them with transit. Except for basic road maintenance, all tolls and gas tax dollars should be diverted to transit projects and urban revitalization. It is important to see the gas tax, in part, as a "sin tax," similar to the tax on alcohol or cigarettes, where part of the proceeds are used to counteract the negative effects of driving. As state politicians look for dedicated funding sources for future busways, light rail, and commuter rail, they must look towards gas taxes and highway tolls as a source of revenue and make the legislative changes that will enable this to happen. This will be politically difficult, but with the will and organization, it is definitely possible.

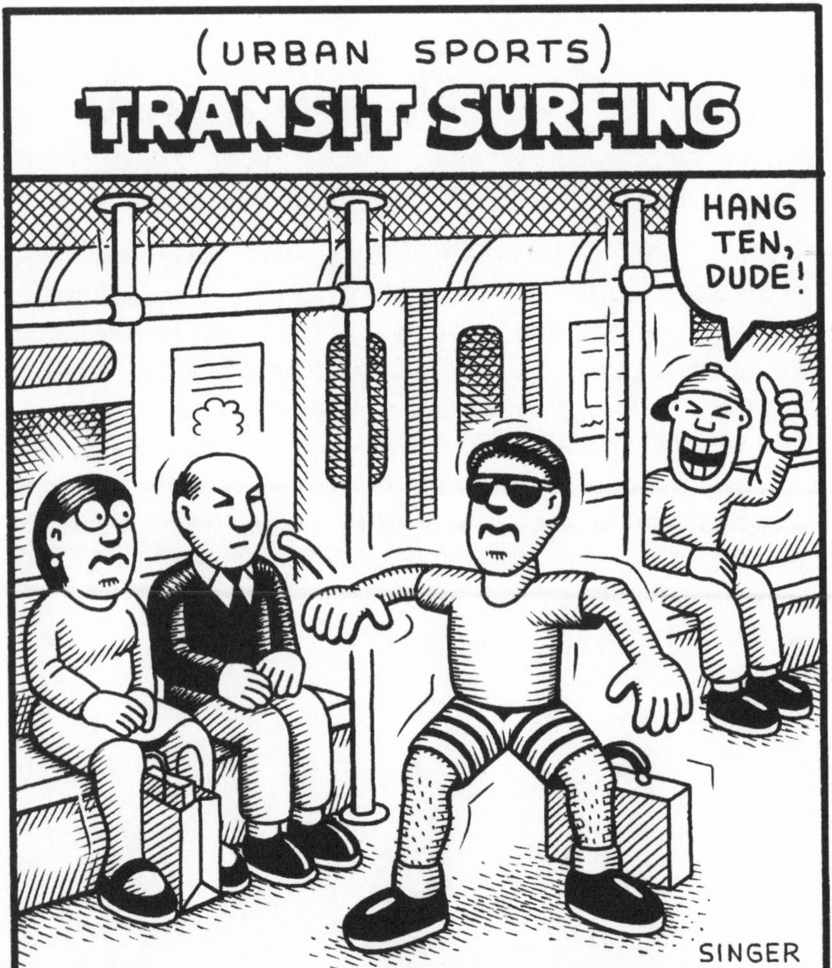
(URBAN SPORTS)
TRANSIT SURFING
HANG TEN, DUDE!
SINGER

Working in our favor is the fact that building and maintaining fixed rail transit provides even more jobs than building highways. With skillful political leadership, a broad array of groups can be led to support transit projects. These include many of the same groups that currently support highways, like unions, construction contractors, heavy industry firms, architecture firms, and groups representing the disabled, the elderly, and voters who are unable to drive.

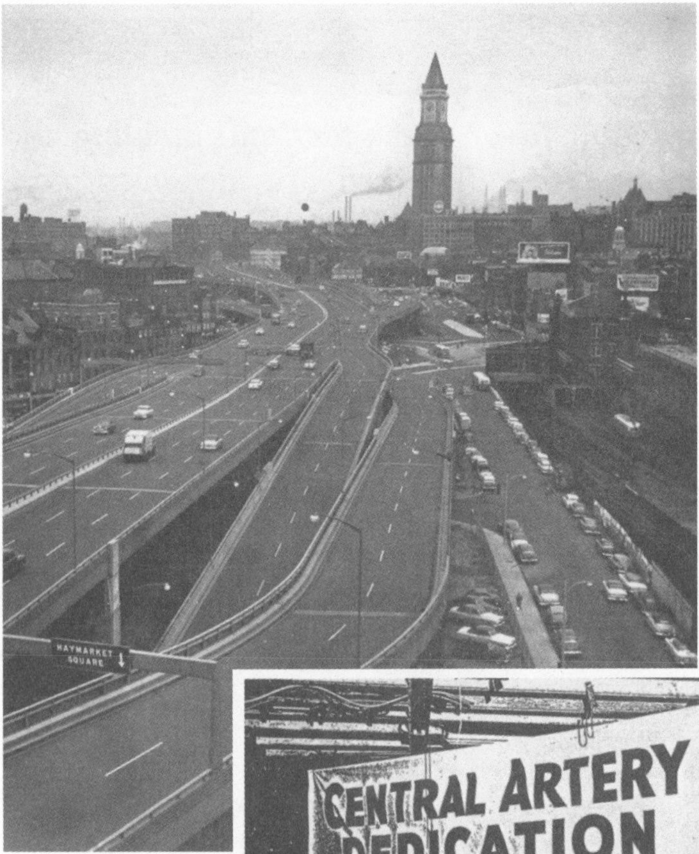
HAYMARKET
SQUARE

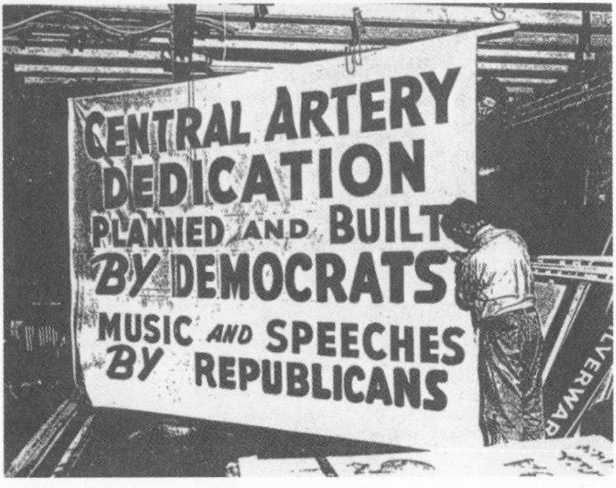
CENTRAL ARTERY
DEDICATION
PLANNED AND BUILT
BY DEMOCRATS
MUSIC AND SPEECHES
BY REPUBLICANS

Making these legislative changes will require educating the public and elected officials. Historically, support for highways has been bipartisan, but from the 1930s until the 1960s, highway agencies were primarily supported by Democrats who viewed highway projects as payback to their trade union constituent base.

These are photographs of the Central Artery freeway that was ripped through the heart of Boston after World War II. Here, Democrats are bragging about constructing it. Ironically, ten years ago, they paid over fifteen billion dollars in construction costs to bury this same short stretch of highway, in a project known simply as "The Big Dig." The Massachusetts Turnpike Authority grossly underestimated the cost of the project, perhaps intentionally. Once the true costs were known, the project was already underway and politicians felt they had no choice but to keep pouring money into it. What began as a 2.8 billion dollar project gradually doubled, then tripled in cost.[32]

In the late 1960s, it was often Republicans who stopped Robert Moses and other highway agencies and revived public transit. People like Nelson Rockefeller, Jr. and Bill Ronan salvaged New York City's bankrupt commuter railroads, and Ronan became the first chairman of New York's MTA. Republicans helped make money available for Bay Area Rapid Transit in San Francisco, Boston's Red Line, AMTRAK, and the rebuilding of dilapidated transit and commuter rail systems in New York, Philadelphia, and many other cities.

32   Central Artery photo courtesy of the Boston Public Library Print Department, Leslie Jones Collection. News photo is from the *Boston Herald*. Both photos taken (with permission) from the late, great Jane Holtz Kay's book <u>Lost Boston</u> (Boston, Mariner Books, a Houghton Mifflin Company, 1999), pg. 311.

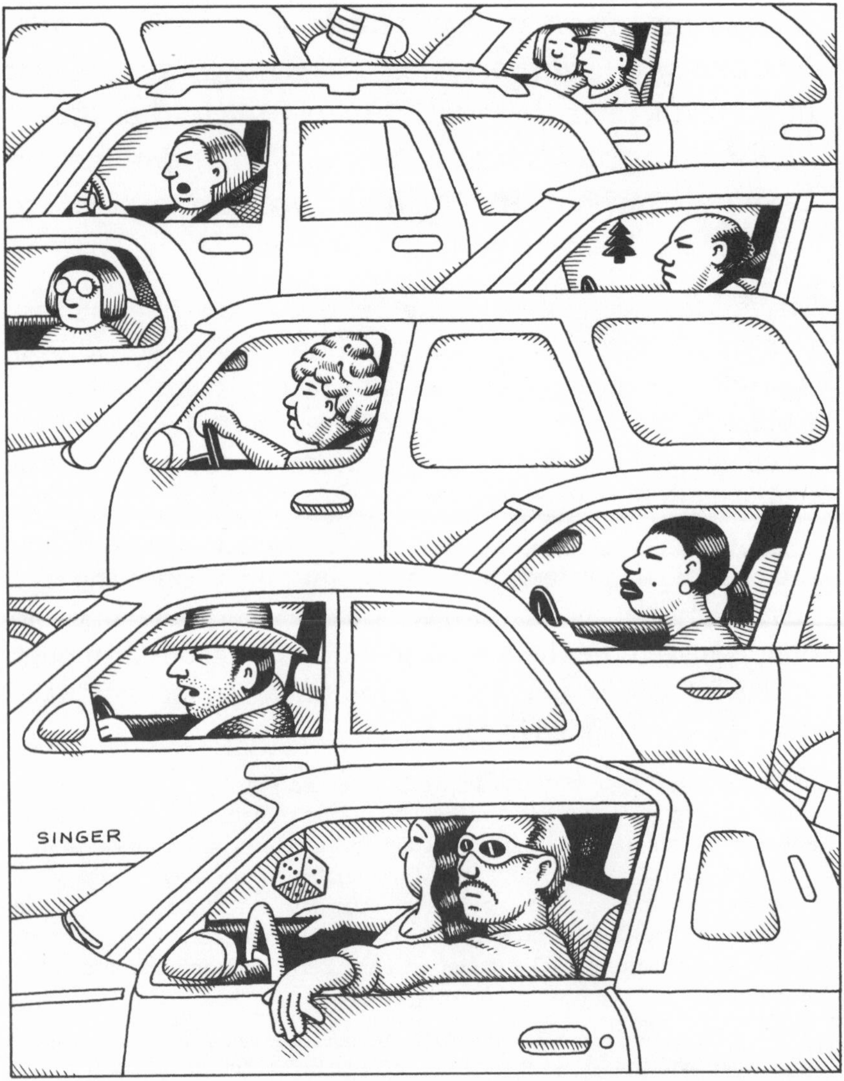
SINGER

In the 1980s and 90s, however, a shift began to take place. The Democratic party's base of support still rested in cities, which had more immigrants, minorities, unions, gays, arts groups, and higher educational institutions. This could be seen in their policies, which focused on stopping urban gun violence, improving health care, education, social welfare, and of course, public transit.

By contrast, Republicans gradually came to represent affluent or middle class suburbanites and exurbanites. These are people who don't use public transit, who don't use as many social services, who don't see urban gun violence and aren't as acutely aware of environmental degradation. Isolated in their cars and single family tract homes, they rarely ever see hardcore urban poverty and rarely meet people different than themselves. They often don't have sidewalks or public transit on which to meet people. They lack access to alternative newspapers, to college radio, to community radio and, in some cases, even to NPR. So the information they receive is more selective. These people support lower taxes and, of course, more highways, so that they can keep driving to their jobs, their strip malls, and their exurban homes. Demographers like Robert Putnam have written about America's decline in "social connectivity" and they believe sprawl, increased driving, and longer commutes are partly responsible.

I call this urban/suburban split "the politics of place"—where you live and how you live influences the way you vote. [33]

---

33   Yonah Freemark, "Understanding the Republican Party's Reluctance to Invest in Transit Infrastructure," *The Transport Politic*, Posted, January 25th, 2011, http://www. thetransportpolitic.com/2011/01/25/understanding-the-republican-partys-reluctance-to-invest-in-transit-infrastructure/

2012 Presidential Election by County

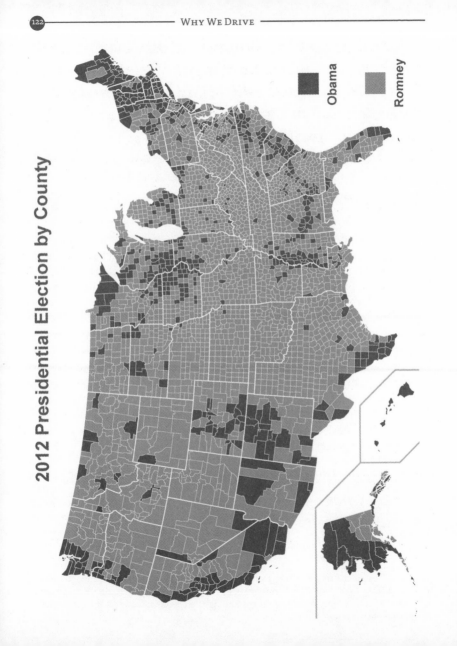

This is a map of the 2012 presidential election by county.[34] The 2008, 2004, and 2000 election maps are almost identical to this one. As you can see, Gore, Kerry, and Obama won most of the cities in the U.S., while Bush, McCain, and Romney won most of the suburbs and exurbs. The exceptions were Indian reservations, some major national parks, and college towns. The latter function much like cities, putting lots of people (students and faculty) close together and giving them access to alternative news and information. If your state still had a majority of its population in urban areas, it went for Obama or a Democrat. If it was suburbanized in the 80s and 90s, like Georgia and Tennessee, it went for Romney or a Republican. The extreme rural areas can vacillate based on farm policies or other issues, but in most states, they represent very few voters. The lion's share of votes are in urban areas or suburban ones, and it's the suburban and exurban voters that Republicans have gone after.

While Europe is still politically urban, the U.S. has become a suburban nation, both physically and in terms of our political values. U.S. citizens have become unilateralist, non-cooperative, oblivious to poverty, environmental degradation, labor, and minority points of view.

Many Democrats don't see and understand this basic fact—that if they don't stop sprawl or greatly curtail it, they will lose cities, lose their base, and lose the war of ideas and culture. During this last economic downturn, many Democrats suggested that we revive the New Deal and make the government a big employer again. As an example of a government project, however, they often suggested more highways. Clearly they don't understand or don't care about the environmental, financial, and demographic issues associated with highways. They need to be educated about them and forced to take action. The fate of cities and the planet depends on it.

34   Map by Kevin Song, made available under the Creative Commons CC0 1.0 Universal Public Domain Dedication, as posted at: http://commons.wikimedia.org/wiki/File:2012_Presidential_Election_by_County.svg

A NONPOLLUTING WEDDING PROCESSION

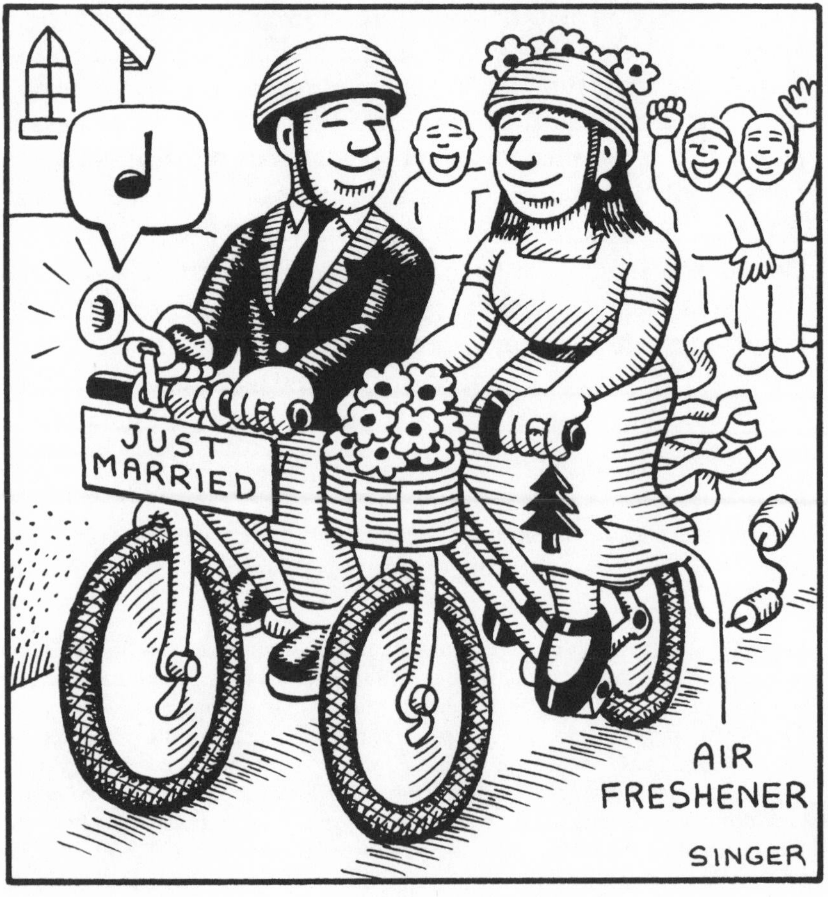
JUST MARRIED
AIR FRESHENER
SINGER

Besides trying to make legislative changes, what can individuals do about all this? How can activists stop the onslaught of cars and highways and promote better urban design and alternative transport?

First there are personal choices: We can choose to live without a car or try to do without one as much as possible. In 47 years, I've never owned a car and I've lived in a lot of places. It just requires some planning when deciding where to live and where to work. You need to situate yourself in an urban or dense suburban area, near bus or transit lines, preferably within walking or biking distance from your job and basic services (groceries, bank, post office, school, etc.). When I absolutely need a car, I rent or borrow one. Now there are even car-sharing companies like Zip Car, and Hour Car, where several people share use of a single car.

Not having a car makes you come up with creative solutions and enables you to see and overcome the influence of car culture on your own life. When my wife and I got married, we had to figure out how to get from the ceremony to the reception and decided to ride bicycles. It was fun but it also made me appreciate how the wedding and funeral industries have managed to make automobile processions a part of our sacred rituals.

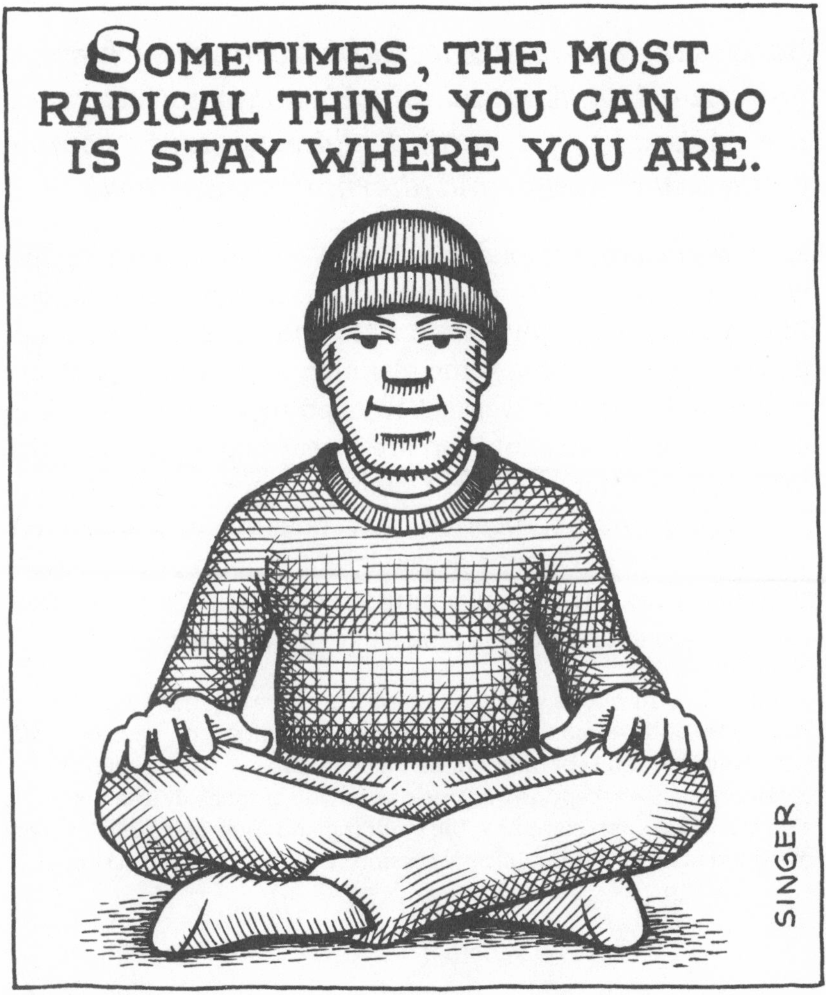
SOMETIMES, THE MOST RADICAL THING YOU CAN DO IS STAY WHERE YOU ARE.
SINGER

Giving up your car seems like a minimal act, but sometimes, not burning hydrocarbons or going anywhere is the most radical thing you can do. This may seem obvious but it's important to realize all the ways our society consciously or unconsciously pressures us to travel. There are advertisements for vacations and travel destinations, pressure to work at places only accessible by car, pressure to purchase larger homes outside of town, and pressure to visit family or friends as frequently as possible. Travel is often presented as a way to make us happier, more relaxed and less lonely. In reality, all this traveling often makes us more stressed out, tired, and isolated.

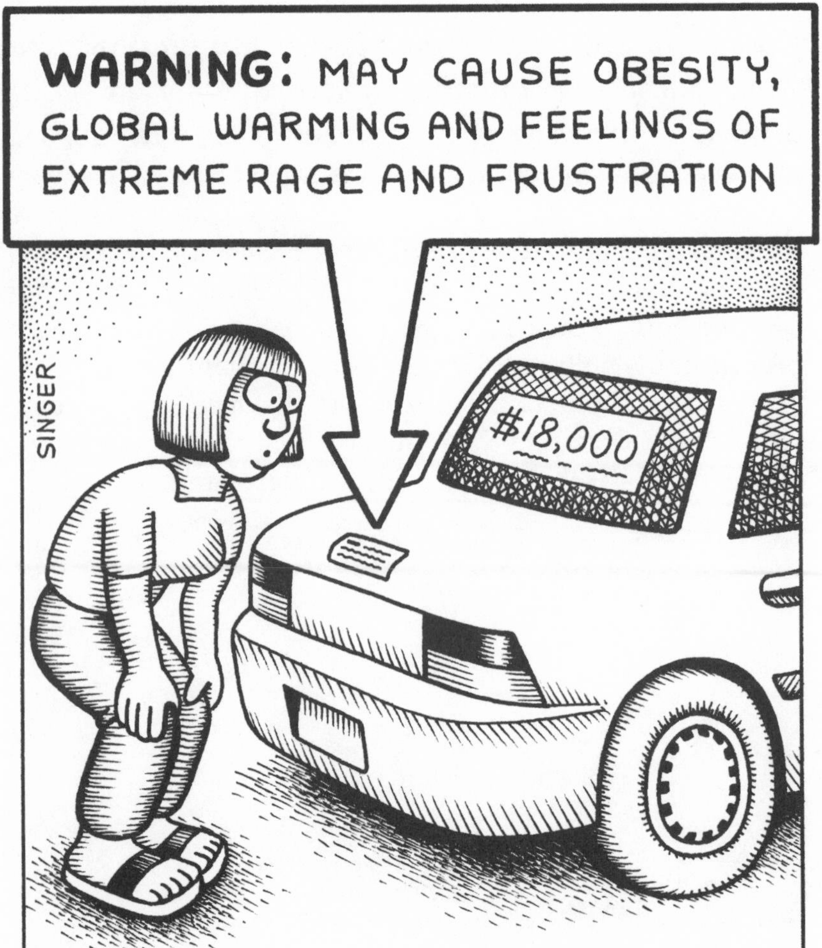
WARNING: MAY CAUSE OBESITY, GLOBAL WARMING AND FEELINGS OF EXTREME RAGE AND FRUSTRATION
SINGER
$18,000

You can try to raise awareness about the problems associated with automobiles by writing, leafletting, blogging, or making art, music, and videos. This was an idea I had for vehicle warning magnets.

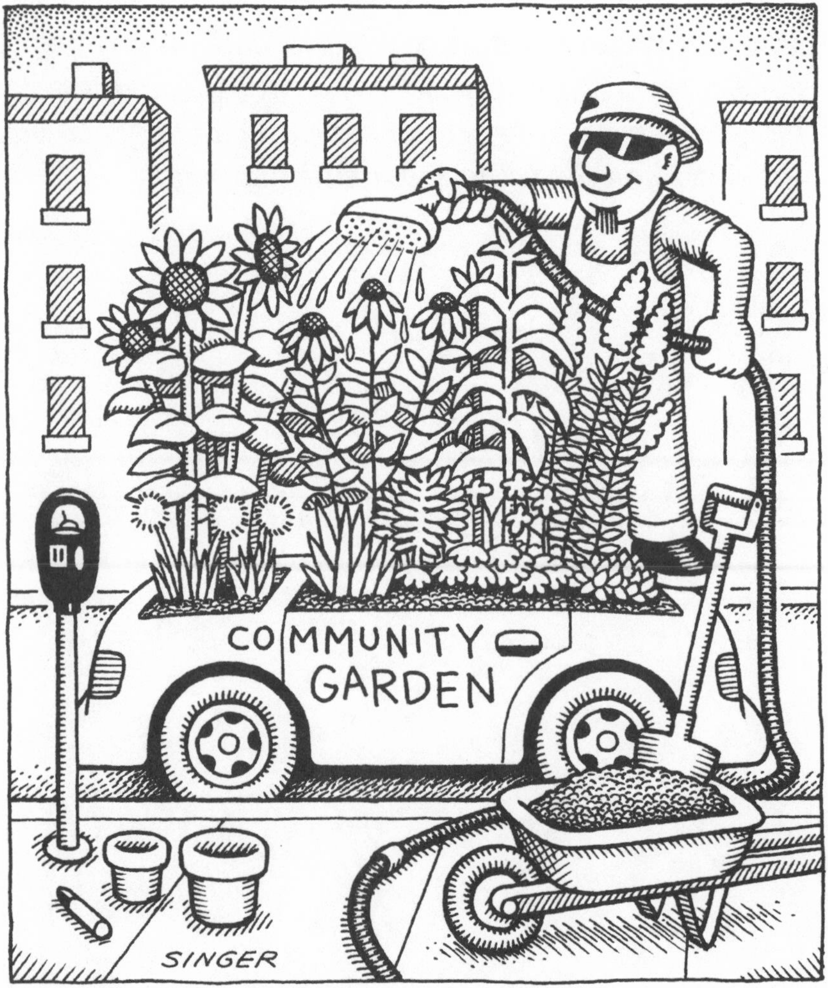
COMMUNITY
GARDEN
SINGER

Or you can create things like this garden car, which people have actually made, to reclaim one parking space at a time. It's fun to make and it's also an educational political statement. Just cut the top off an old car, gut the inside, fill it with dirt and plant a garden. Then drag it to a parking space. Don't forget to put money in the meter!

Many cities are also starting to allow sidewalk extension platforms in parking spaces. These wooden or metal platforms can extend a curb and reclaim a parking space for outdoor café seating, bike racks, planters, or benches.

Some cities celebrate "Park(ing) Day" or hold "Open Streets" events where games, meals and parties occur in temporarily reclaimed streets or parking places.

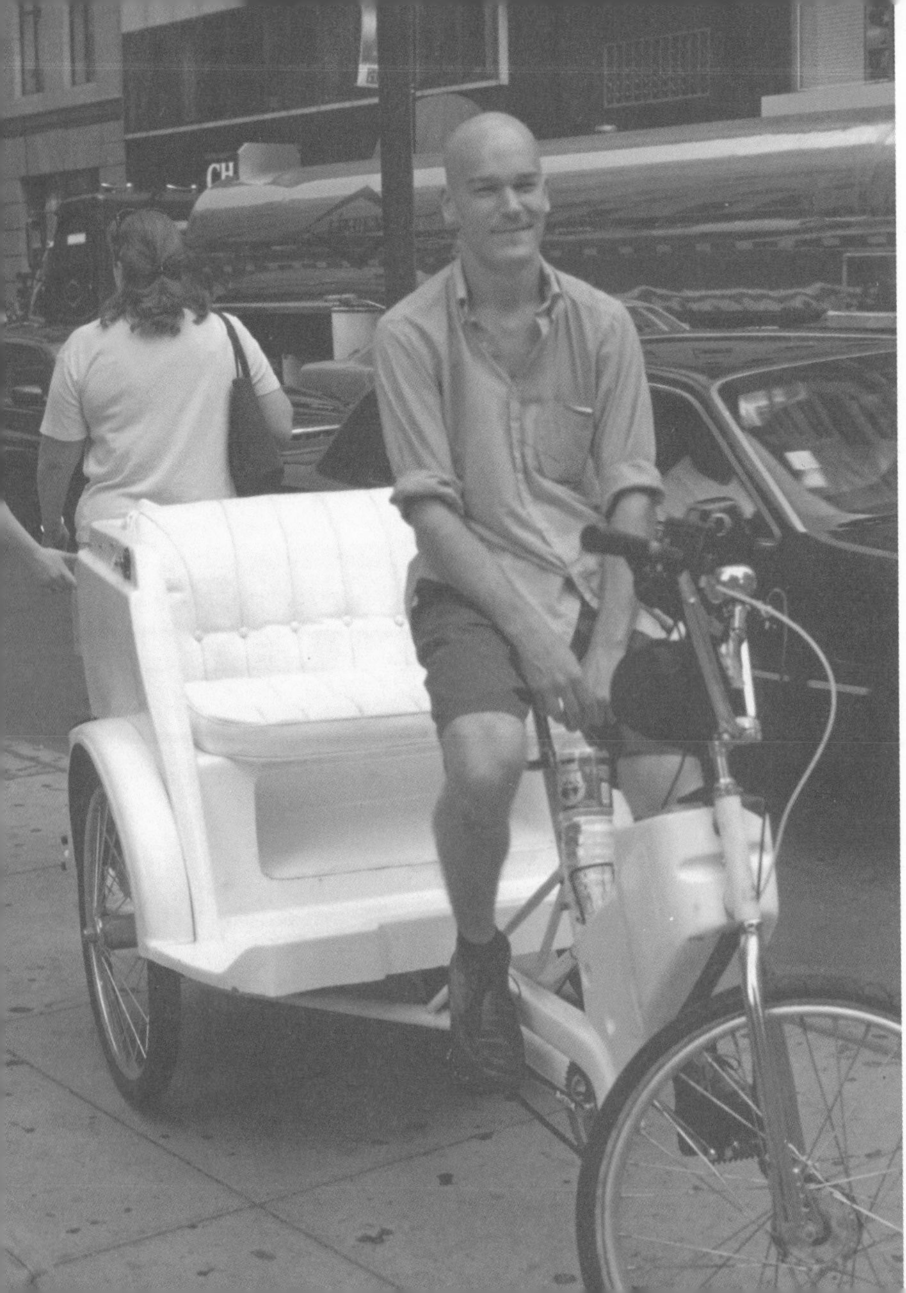

You can start alternative transport businesses, like PEDEX in Berkeley, California, which delivers packages and goods in big hauler bicycles or like this pedal powered taxi in New York City. And you can patronize and support these businesses, especially when they are being challenged by motorized taxi and limousine companies. There are around 1,500 pedicabs operating just in New York City. That's 1,500 fewer motorized taxis belching out smog and CO_2! Given New York's insane traffic, pedicabs can often get you to your destination faster than regular taxis.

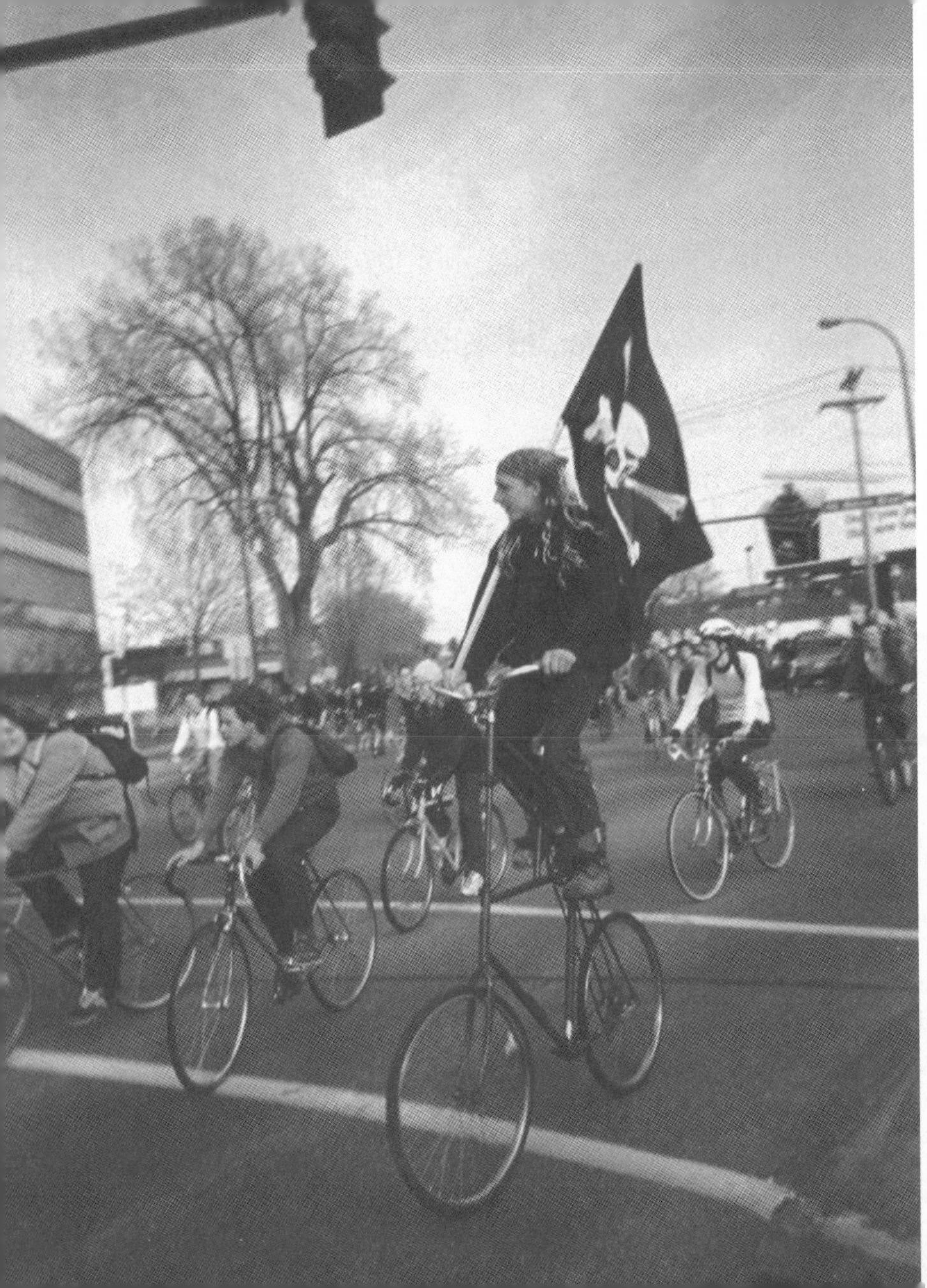

Or you can participate in mass group activities, like this Critical Mass bike ride in Minneapolis, Minnesota. In many cities, Critical Mass is a monthly event where bicyclists meet up at some designated area in mass and then ride wherever they want. Its slogan is "We are traffic." Massers have run into conflicts with police, but in Minneapolis and other cities we have won the right to ride by bringing political pressure on the mayor and city council.

Critical mass rides have helped bring more attention to bicycles and they're a great way to meet other cyclists and have fun.

ORGANIZE A PEDAL POWERED PARADE !
SINGER

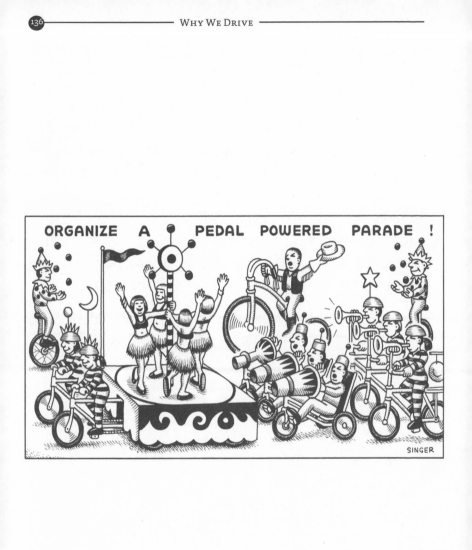

If a city refuses to allow Critical Mass rides and demands order and permits, you can organize big public festivals or pedal-powered parades.

Numerous cities have "Art Car" parades. Why not "Art Bike" parades?

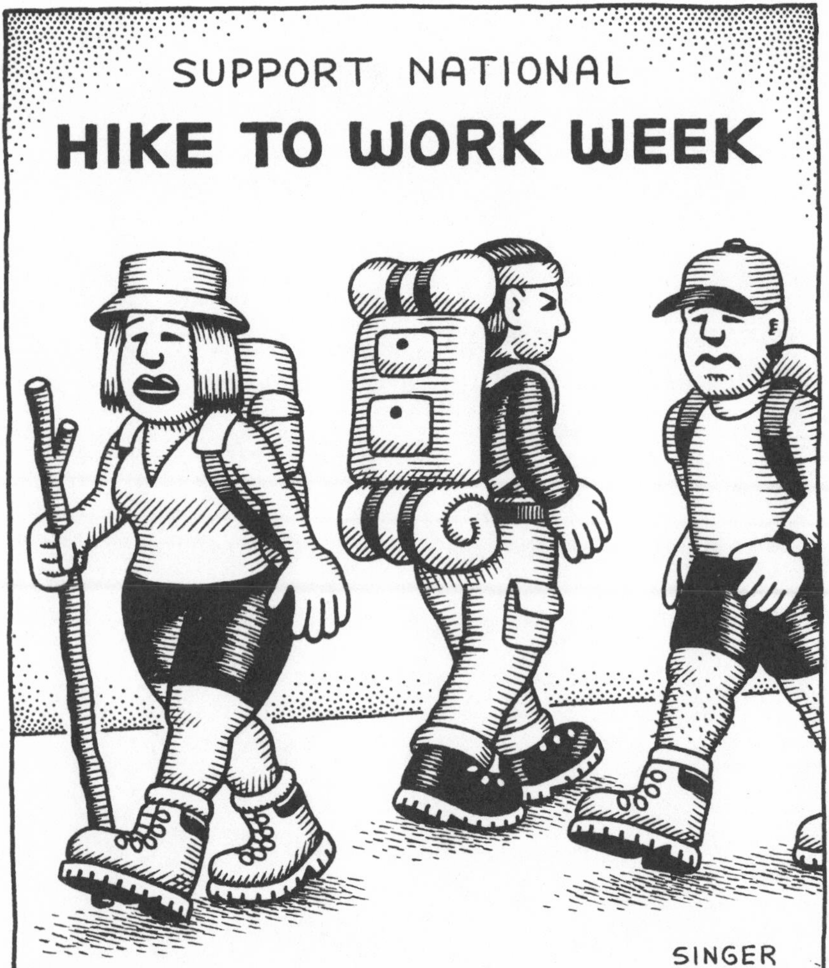
SUPPORT NATIONAL
HIKE TO WORK WEEK
SINGER

Or you can organize city-wide awareness events and get your elected officials to participate, just to experience life without a car and see what their city looks like on foot.

Many local politicians perpetuate car-oriented transportation planning and land use, not out of malice but because they have no idea what it's like to traverse their city without a car. They often don't realize how much of a barrier a highway or big boulevard poses to pedestrians and how this might be hurting businesses or negatively impacting their city. Taking them on walking, biking, or transit tours of their city or getting them to bike or walk to work can make them see the need for transit or pedestrian improvements.

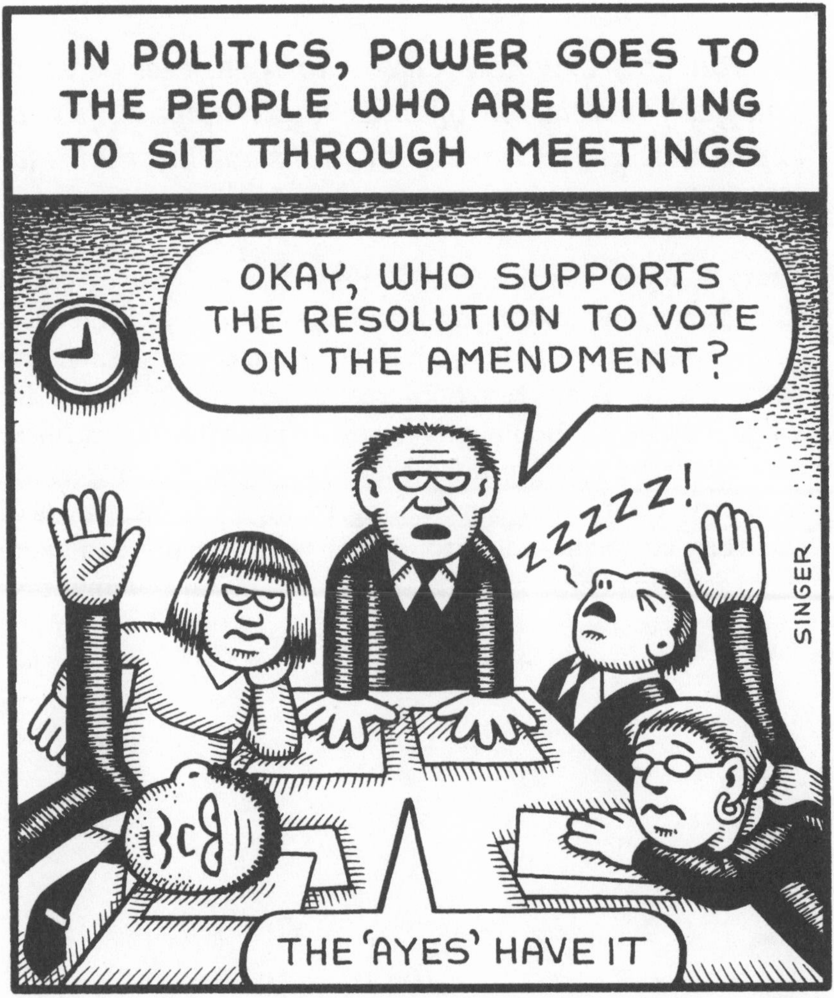
IN POLITICS, POWER GOES TO THE PEOPLE WHO ARE WILLING TO SIT THROUGH MEETINGS
OKAY, WHO SUPPORTS THE RESOLUTION TO VOTE ON THE AMENDMENT?
ZZZZZZ!
THE 'AYES' HAVE IT
SINGER

At some point, however, you must participate in the political process. There is no substitute for making major legislative changes. Meetings are no fun, but political power goes to those who are willing to sit through meetings. Your local zoning boards, community councils, and metropolitan planning organizations can have a big impact on urban design and transportation choices. I encourage people to pay attention to these organizations and become active on transportation issues.

There are also lots of groups trying to push transit, cycling, and walking. At a national level groups like Project for Public Spaces, T4America, Bikes Belong, and dozens of others are doing good work. At the local level, most cities have bicycle coalitions and groups for pedestrian and public transit advocacy. I've listed a few of them in the back of this book.

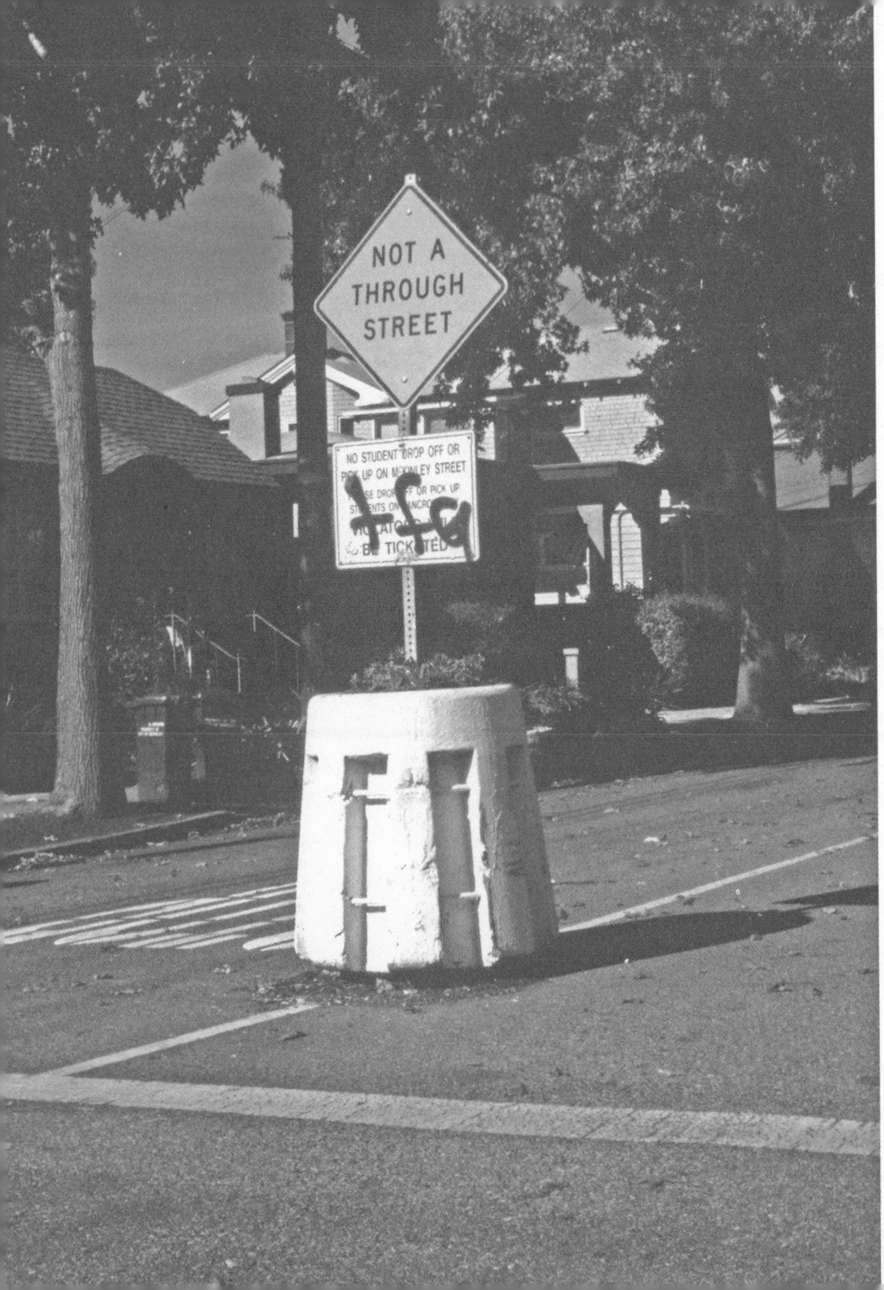
NOT A
THROUGH
STREET
NO STUDENT DROP OFF OR
PICK UP ON McKINLEY STREET

Through politics—collective community action— you can get bollards like this one, to temporarily or permanently block off your street to thru-traffic. This allows kids to play in the street and reclaims a big piece of public space from automobiles.

Or you can get more elaborate street planters like this one in Berkeley, California.

It's located on a long east-west street that was designated a "bicycle boulevard." Barriers at various points along the street, like this planter, prevent thru car traffic but allow bicycles and emergency vehicles to pass. This reduces and slows car traffic and creates a safer environment for cyclists and pedestrians. Creation of these bike boulevards and other traffic calming measures also tend to boost real estate values and increase interaction among neighbors.

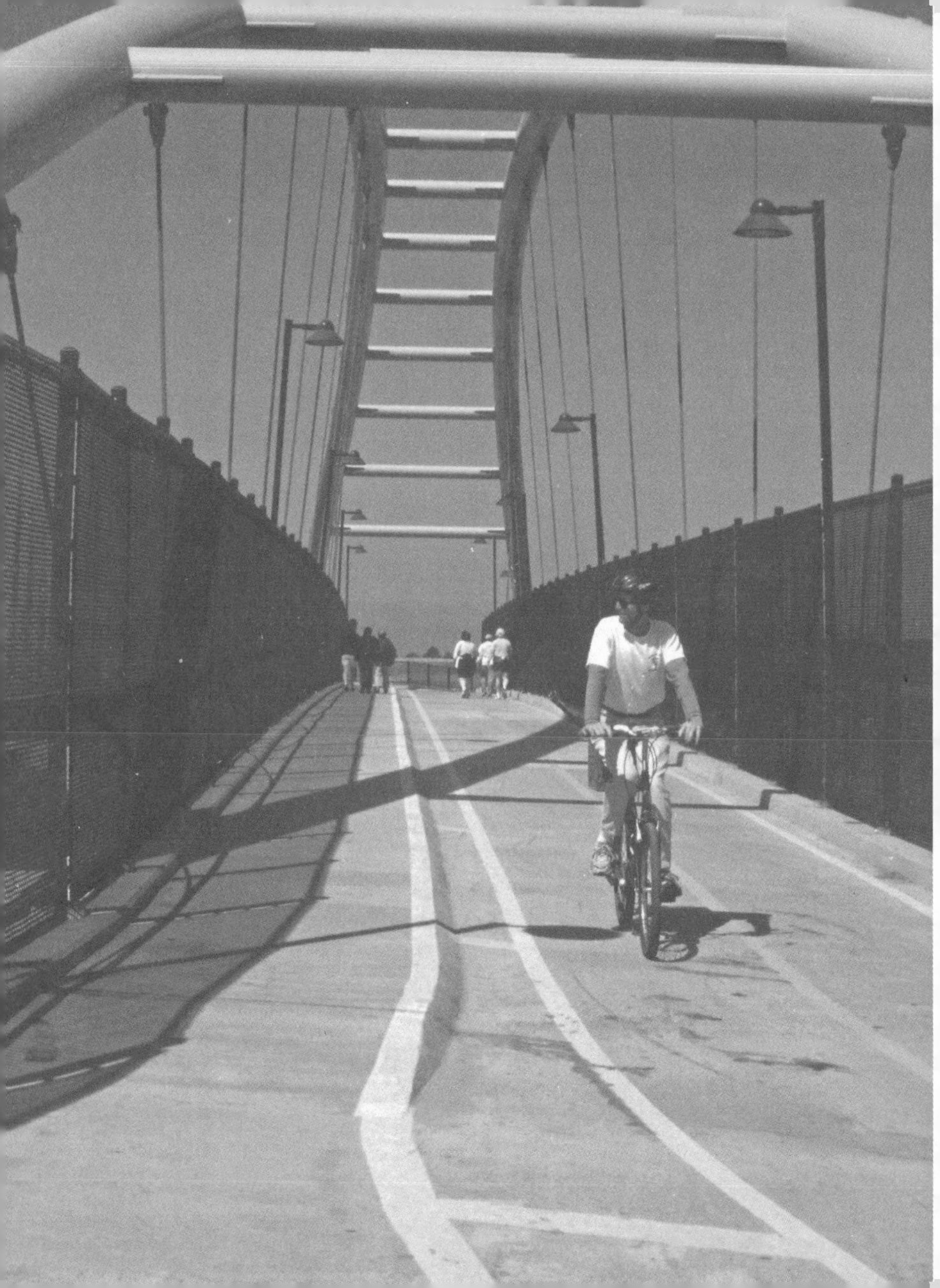

Through politics, you can get bike or pedestrian bridges over highways, railroads or other urban obstacles. This one traverses Interstate 80 in Berkeley, California and helped to revitalize the city's marina and shoreline parks.

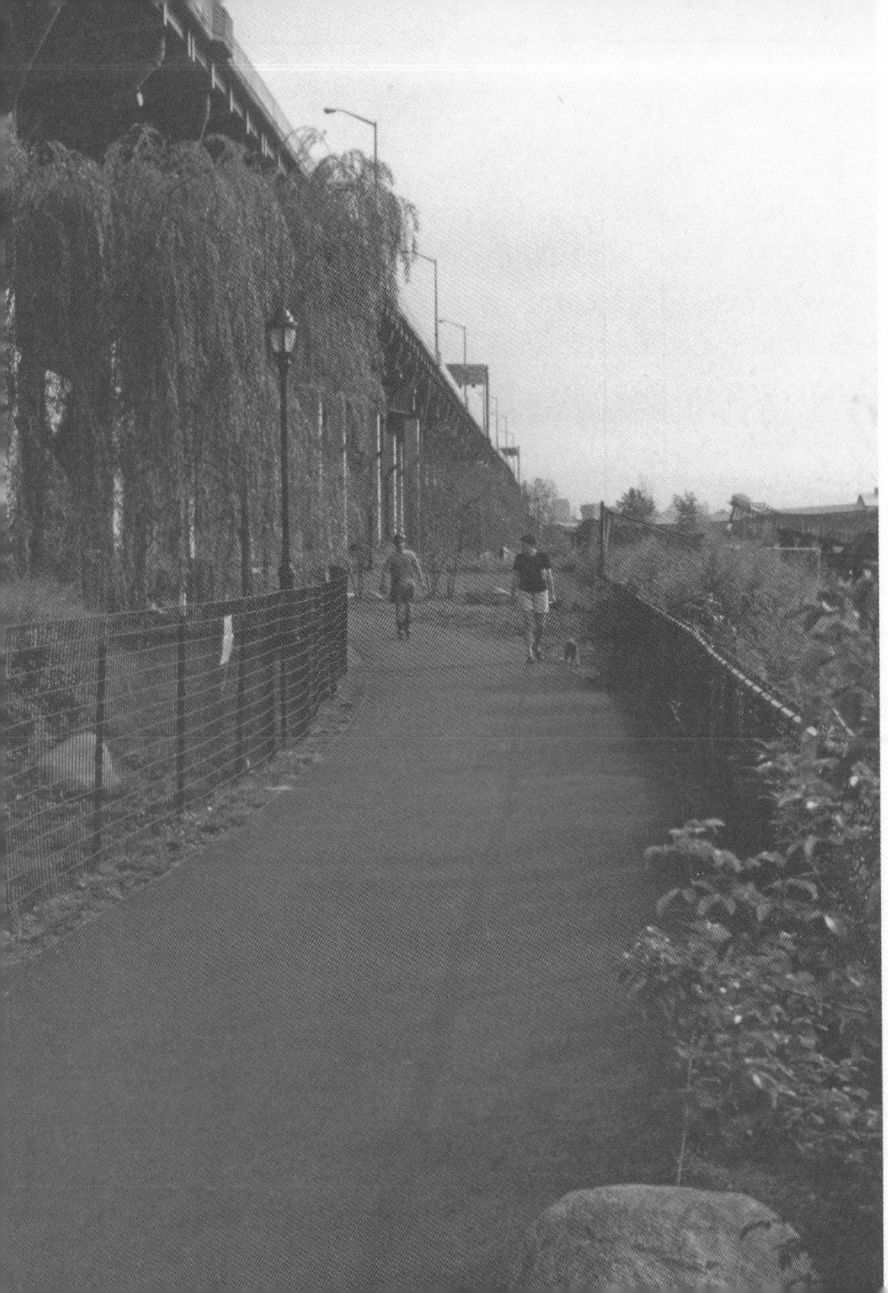

Or, you can create things like the Hudson River Greenway— an incredible project that was brought about by sustained political pressure from many groups in New York City over many years. It extends from the south end of Riverside Park and 72nd street, all the way to Battery Park and the tip of Manhattan.

These photographs were taken on a Sunday evening, but on weekdays, the Greenway is full of bike commuters who can now safely bicycle down almost the entire length of Manhattan Island without having to compete for space with cars.

On the left is another view of the Hudson River Greenway, looking south. For a minute, you forget you're in the middle of New York City.

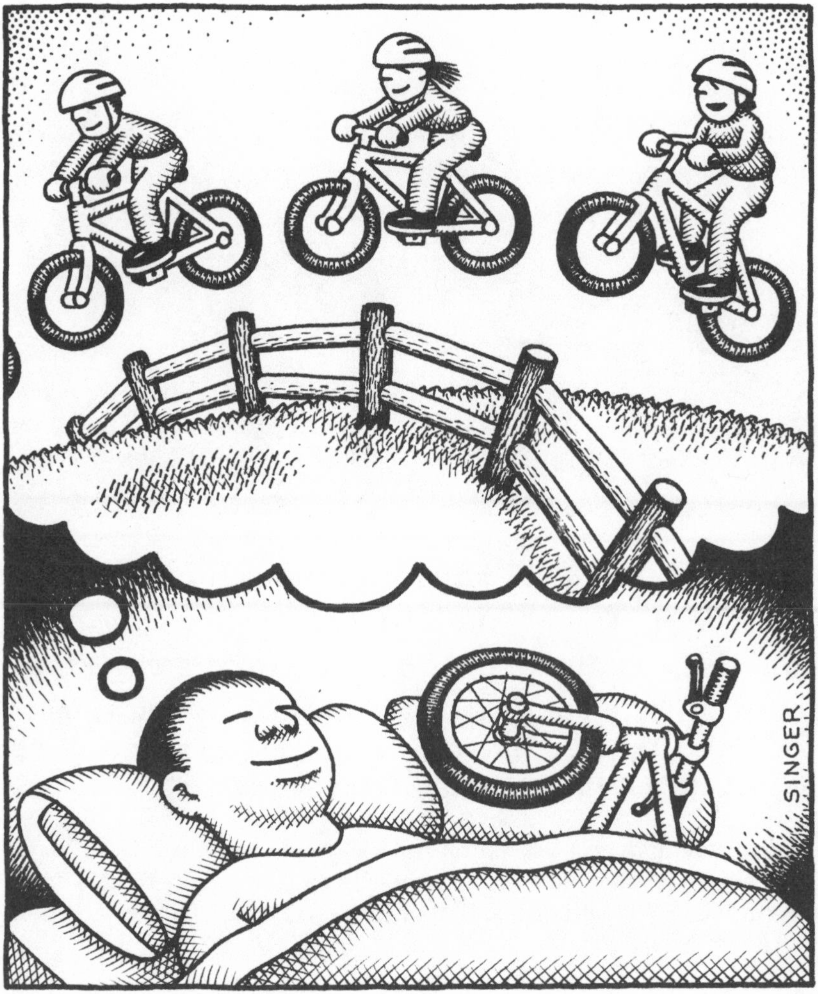
SINGER

Through politics and commandeering a greater share of federal and state gas taxes and motor vehicle fees, you can get better transit, urban revitalization, and maybe even a complete ban on private cars in city sections or one day, entire cities.

As I said at the beginning of this book, I believe that creating one large car-free section of an American city would be a powerful example of what's possible. It would prove to people that it could be done and would show how eliminating cars could improve quality of life, improve the environment, and reduce American dependence on foreign oil. If you dream big, organize, and ask for what you want, you just might get it.

BIBLIOGRAPHY:

Caro, Robert. *The Power Broker: Robert Moses and the Fall of New York*. New York: Vintage Books, 1974.
A Pulitzer Prize winning biography that gives an unparalleled look into the inner workings of a city and state highway authority. The book examines the political and economic power bases of highway agencies, how they wield that power and efforts (both successful and unsuccessful) to fight them.

Downs, Anthony. *Stuck in Traffic: Coping with Peak-Hour Traffic Congestion*. Washington, DC: The Brookings Institution, 1992.
This book gives a detailed analysis of traffic congestion and, one by one, looks at all of the various proposed solutions. I like its idea of "100 small cuts." Alas, it does not consider larger environmental implications of proposed solutions.

Goddard, Stephen. *Getting There: The epic struggle between road and rail in the American century*. New York: Basic Books, 1994.
A historical analysis of why automobiles succeeded and American passenger rail and public transportation failed.

Illich, Ivan. *Energy and Equity*. London: Calder and Boyars Ltd., 1974.
One of the most creative, thoughtful little essays you will ever read—a bicycling and pedestrian manifesto. It considers the failings of modern transport and the relationship between a society's energy use and its level of social equity.

Kay, Jane Holtz. *Asphalt Nation: How the Automobile Took Over America and How We Can Take It Back*. Berkeley, California: University of California Press, 1997.
An excellent and thorough analysis of the history and impact of cars in the United States, with particular focus on the way they have impacted architectural and urban space.

Kitman, Jamie Lincoln. "The Secret History of Lead." *The Nation* 270 (20 March 2000): 11-44.
A thoroughly researched and well written history of the collusion between General Motors, Standard Oil, and Du Pont to make and market leaded gasoline—a deadly poison still sold in countries all over the world.

Marrin, Albert. _Black Gold: The Story of Oil in Our Lives_. New York: Knopf, 2012.
Despite being for younger readers, this book is a great overview history of oil uses, discoveries, exploration, and exploitation. I particularly liked the sections on Rockefeller and urban areas during the horse-drawn era.

Pushkarev, Boris S. and Jeffrey Zupan. _Public Transportation and Land Use Policy_. Bloomington, Indiana: Indiana University Press, 1977.
Based on studies prepared for the New York Tri-State Regional Planning Commission, this book considers what conditions of population density, fare price, frequency and travel time will enable different forms of public transport to be successful. It is fairly technical but features a brief, extremely interesting history of urban density, from ancient Egypt to the present day.

Putnam, Robert D. _Bowling Alone: The Collapse and Revival of American Community_. New York: Touchstone, 2000.
Putnam quanitifies America's decline in civic engagement and social connectivity over the last 50-100 years and tries to desipher its various causes. The chapter on Mobility and Sprawl will be of particular interest to transportation activists. I wondered if some of the other causes Putnam attributes to the decline (like "Generational Differences") are also impacted by sprawl or the physical environment in which people are raised.

St. Clair, David, _The Motorization of American Cities_. New York: Praeger Publishers, 1986.
Gives a detailed account of National City Lines, American City Lines, and Pacific City Lines take overs and conversions of urban trolley networks to buses.

Transportation Research Board, Transit Cooperative Research Program Report 129: Local and Regional Funding Mechanisms for Public Transportation. Washington DC: www.TRB.org, 2009. An analysis of current and potential ways in which states and cities finance public transit, with guidance for drafting and enacting new funding mechanisms. Available for download at: http://onlinepubs.trb.org/onlinepubs/tcrp/tcrp_rpt_129.pdf

Weingroff, Richard. "Creating a Landmark: The intermodal Surface Transportation Act of 1991." _Public Roads_ Vol. 65, No. 3 (Nov/Dec 2001): http://www.fhwa.dot.gov/publications/publicroads/01novdec/istea.cfm
(Also a telephone interview with Mr. Weingroff on March 8, 2013).

ALTERNATIVE TRANSPORT GROUPS AND RESOURCES:

The following are just a few of the hundreds of bicycle, pedestrian and transit organizations in the U.S. with which I've had some personal interaction.

AMERICA WALKS
A national coalition of local advocacy groups promoting walkable communities, assisting community pedestrian groups and educating the public.
PO Box 10581
Portland, OR 97296
tel: (503) 757-8342
e-mail: sbricker@americawalks.org
web: http://www.americawalks.org/

AMERICAN FARMLAND TRUST
Works to stop the loss of productive farmland and to promote farming practices that lead to a healthy environment.
1200 18th Street, NW, Suite 800
Washington, DC 20036
tel: (202) 331-7300
e-mail: info@farmland.org
web: http://www.farmland.org/

AMERICAN PUBLIC TRANSPORT ASSOCIATION
Membership organization for U.S. transit providers. Publishes *Coalition Building Workbook* and many other guides and reports on-line and in print form. Website has useful information and links to state and local transit advocacy groups.
1666 K Street NW, Suite 1100
Washington, DC 20006
tel: (202) 496-4800
web: http://www.apta.com/

BICYCLE TRANSPORTATION ALLIANCE (BTA)
Portland, Oregon's cycling advocates, "Creating safe, sane, and sustainable communities, one bike at a time."
618 NW Glisan Street #401
Portland, OR 97209
tel: (503) 226-0676
e-mail: Greer@BTAOregon.org
web: http://BTAOregon.org/

BIKE TEXAS
Advancing Bicycle Access, Safety and Education.
1902 East 6th
Austin, TX 78702
tel: (512) 476-RIDE (7433)
e-mail: mail@biketexas.org
web: http://www.biketexas.org/

CENTER FOR APPROPRIATE TRANSPORT
Cycling and pedestrian advocacy group that builds work bikes, recumbents and trailers; provides youth bike education and training.
455 West 1st Avenue
Eugene, OR 97401
tel: (541) 344-1197
e-mail: cat@catoregon.org/
web: http://www.catoregon.org/

ACTIVE TRANSPORTATION ALLIANCE
Formerly Chicagoland Bicycle Federation, ATA promotes biking, walking and transit in Chicago.
9 W. Hubbard Street, Suite 402
Chicago, IL 60654-6545
tel: (312) 427-3325 (42-PEDAL)
e-mail: cbf@biketraffic.org
web: http://www.activetrans.org/

CONGRESS FOR THE NEW URBANISM
The New Urbanism movement seeks to reform all aspects of real estate development and promote denser walkable communities with a mix of jobs and housing.
The Marquette Building
140 S. Dearborn St., Suite 404
Chicago, IL 60603
tel: (312) 551-7300
e-mail: cnuinfo@cnu.org
web: http://www.cnu.org/

EAST BAY BICYCLE COALITION
Promotes bicycling as an everyday means of transportation and recreation. Fights for bicycle access on public transit, city streets and bridges. Provides free, secure bicycle parking at popular public events.
P.O. Box 1736
Oakland, CA 94604
tel: (510) 845-RIDE (7433)
web: http://www.ebbc.org/

INSTITUTE FOR TRANSPORTATION
& DEVELOPMENT POLICY
A leader in developing and implementing green transport policy in the developing world.
9 East 19th Street, 7th Floor
New York, NY 10003
tel: (212) 629-8001
e-mail: mobility@itdp.org
web: http://www.itdp.org/

LEAGUE OF AMERICAN BICYCLISTS
National bike education, advocacy and lobby group; Sponsors National Bike Month and Bike-to-Work Day; Certifies Bicycle Friendly Communities and Businesses; Web site links to state/local bike groups throughout the U.S.
1612 K Street NW, Suite 510
Washington, DC 20006,
tel: (202) 822-1333
web: http://www.bikeleague.org/

NATIONAL ASSOCIATION OF RAILROAD PASSENGERS
Promotes intercity passenger rail service in the U.S. Offers fare discounts and info to train travelers.
505 Capitol Court, NE, Suite 300
Washington, DC 20002-7706
tel: (202) 408-8362
e-mail: narp@narprail.org
web: http://www.narprail.org/

PENTRANS
Works to create public and private support for sufficient dedicated public transportation funding in Pennsylvania. Produces an excellent e-mail newsletter with transportation related stories from Pennsylvania and around the nation.
1435 Walnut Street, Suite 3
Philadelphia, PA 19102
tel: (215) 205-8157
e-mail: info@pentrans.org
web: http://www.pentrans.org/

PROJECT FOR PUBLIC SPACES
Works with local groups, agencies and governments to establish healthy public spaces, often by taking space away from automobiles.
419 Lafayette Street, Seventh Floor
New York, NY 10003
tel: (212) 620-5660
e-mail: info@pps.org
web: http://www.pps.org/

RAILS-TO-TRAILS CONSERVANCY
Works with local communities to convert abandoned railroad lines into public pathways for non-automotive transportation.
The Duke Ellington Building
2121 Ward Court NW, 5th Floor
Washington, DC 20037
tel: (202) 331-9696
web: http://www.railtrails.org/

SAN FRANCISCO
BICYCLE COALITION
Bicycle advocacy group "dedicated to making San Francisco the most bike-friendly city in the Nation."
833 Market Street, 10th Floor
San Francisco, CA 94103
tel: (415) 431-BIKE (2453)
e-mail: info@sfbike.org
web: http://www.sfbike.org/

STREETSBLOG.ORG
A daily news source for information on sustainable transportation and livable communities with contributors in New York, San Francisco, Chicago, Los Angeles, Washington DC and around the country. Originally created by Aaron Naparstek and others in New York, and produced by OpenPlans, it has tons of ideas, data, studies, articles, films, and much more.

TRANSIT FOR LIVABLE COMMUNITIES
Advocates for public transit funding and expansion in the state of Minnesota. They were also administrators of a 28 million dollar Federal non-motorized pilot project, largely in Minneapolis, that invested heavily in bicycle and pedestrian infrastructure to see how much it would increase rates of biking and walking.
2356 University Avenue, Suite 403
Saint Paul, MN 55114
tel: (651) 767-0298
e-mail: tlc@tlcminnesota.org
web: http://www.tlcminnesota.org/

TRANSPORTATION ALTERNATIVES
New York City's advocates for cyclists, pedestrians and public transportation. Publishes an excellent quarterly newsletter. Responsible for Streetsblog and many other innovations in alternative transportation advocacy, media, mapping, and much more.
127 West 26th Street, Suite 1002
New York, NY 10001
tel: (212) 629-8080
e-mail: info@transalt.org
web: http://www.transalt.org/

TRANSPORTATION FOR AMERICA
National lobby organization pushing for transportation spending reform and greater investment in public transit and non-motorized transportation.
1707 L Street NW, Suite 250
Washington, DC 20036
tel: (202) 955-5543
e-mail: info@t4america.org
Web: http://t4america.org/

VICTORIA TRANSPORT POLICY INSTITUTE
Independent research organization dedicated to developing innovative and practical tools for solving transportation problems. Provides a wide range of studies, guides and software, most available for free on its website. Its *Transit Demand Management Encyclopedia* is great as are some of their reports.
1250 Rudlin Street
Victoria, BC, V8V 3R7, Canada
tel: +1(250) 360-1560
e-mail: info@vtpi.org
web: http://www.vtpi.org/

WILDLANDS CENTER FOR PREVENTING ROADS
Works to protect and restore wildland ecosystems by preventing and removing roads and limiting motorized recreation on public land. Clearinghouse on wilderness road impacts and road-fighting strategies. Publishes *Road RIPorter*.
P.O. Box 7516
Missoula, MT 59807
Tel: (406) 543-9551
web: http://www.wildlandscpr.org/